Trencherman's Gu

Best Inns & _ _ in the South East

Compiled by: Gordon Dunkerley
John Wilson
Mervyn Woodward

Edited by: James Lawrence

CONTENTS

Important 2
Surrey 3
Hampshire 19
Sussex 45
Kent 76
Locator Maps 100
Index 102

This book is published quite independently of any brewery or group of public houses, and has no connection with any company of a similar name.

Published by
Bracken Publishing
Bracken House, 199a Holt Road
Cromer, Norfolk NR 27 9JN

Copyright © Bracken Publishing. All rights reserved.

ISBN 1 871614 15 5

Printed by Broadgate Printers, Aylsham, Norfolk.

March 1993

Introduction

Please note:-

1. *Dishes quoted from menus are examples only, and not necessarily available at all times.*

2. *The listing of brewers' beers and lagers does not mean that their full range is necessarily available.*

3. *Prices, where quoted, may alter during the currency of this guide.*

4. *Every effort is made to ensure accuracy, but inevitably circumstances alter and errors and omissions occur. Therefore the publisher cannot accept liability for any consequences arising therefrom.*

5. *This is a selection: it is not claimed that all the best inns and pubs are featured.*

6. *Your comments about any establishment, favourable or not, are particularly welcome. Correspondents who especially impress the editor will receive a complimentary copy of the next edition.*

7. *Special note to publicans: if your house is not included, please do not be offended! The area covered is large, and time limited. If you serve good food in pleasant surrounds, please write and we will visit you.*

FURTHER COPIES OF THIS OR OUR OTHER GUIDES MAY BE OBTAINED BY WRITING TO:-

Bracken Publishing
Bracken House
199a Holt Road
Cromer
Norfolk NR27 9JN

Other guides:-

Eastern Counties	£4.00
Eastern Counties Hotels & Restaurants	£3.50
Cotswolds, Thames Valley & Chilterns	£3.50
Midlands	£3.50
West Country	£3.50

Prices include postage etc. No orders will be accepted without prior payment, other than from book retailers.

SURREY

THE HAYCUTTER

Tanhouse Road, Broadham Green, nr Oxted.　　　　　　Tel. (0883) 712550
　　　Location:　On village green, south of old Oxted.
　Credit cards:　Not accepted.
　　　　Bitters:　Friary Meux, John Bull, Youngs, Tetley, Burton.
　　　　Lagers:　Lowenbrau, Skol, Castlemaine.

Examples of bar/restaurant meals (lunch & evening, Mon - Sat): *lobster bisque, scallops provencale, avocado & chicken salad, dressed crab salad, plaice stuffed with prawns & mushrooms, veal cordon bleu, lamb chops, grilled sardines, fresh fish, steaks, ploughman's, sandwiches, daily specials. Complimentary bar nibbles on Sundays. Fresh desserts.*

Catering is a demanding profession (imagine throwing a dinner party for umpteen guests, 12 times per week); an unforgiving public remembers only the last meal, and if it was not up to expectations one stands condemned for ever, so it is sheer consistency that is the keynote of this successful country pub, quietly situated by the village green. All is fresh and cooked to order, and always of a high standard - fish and steaks are especially noted - and accompanied by a good wine list. One may dine in the single bar or separate restaurant (children welcome), amidst the old beams and an unusual collection of regimental hats. A skittles alley can be reserved for parties and meetings, with food laid on, and barbecues are arranged occasionally in season in the large garden. Barry Aldridge, daughter Sheelagh and staff are on hand with a cordial greeting. Ample parking.

THE WOODCOCK INN

Woodcock Hill, Felbridge.   Tel. (0342) 325859

          Location: North of village on A22.
      Credit cards: Access, Visa.
  Accommodation: 2 doubles (£35), 2 suites (£55 & £65). TV's, 'phones, breakfast in rooms. Special rates on request.
           Bitters: Larkins, Gibbs, Exmoor, Harveys Armada, Ringwood.
            Lagers: Fosters, Holsten Export.

Examples of bar meals (lunch & evening, 7 days): *wild duck in red wine, chicken Kiev, moussaka, steaks, mixed shellfish, ploughman's, sandwiches, daily specials, cold buffet in summer.*
Examples of restaurant meals (as above - booking advised weekends): *selection of fresh fish (displayed), hot croissant filled with shellfish, game in season, maigret of duck, calves liver grilled with bacon & sage, lobster, chef's specials, extensive choice for Sunday lunch.*

"Good food is an art", says landlady Valerie Jones on her menu - her creations have won very high ratings for her characterful 15th century inn in a leading national good pub guide. Flexibility is a key word; everyone is treated as an individual, and menus tailored to suit. Fresh fish is the forte, including some quite uncommon, such as pike. Also very uncommon are the furnishings; upholstered milk churns as bar stools, lacquered oriental benches, fancy fans and parasols are amongst a host of collectables and antiques. A black spiral staircase leads to a candlelit gallery and function room for 100, and on to a Victorian style dining room, bookable for private parties up to 18. Children are welcome, and there is a patio.

Surrey

THE BELL INN

Outwood Lane, Outwood, nr Redhill.　　　　Tel. (0342) 842989/844427
　　　　Location:　Next to windmill on Smallfield to Bletchingly road.
　　Credit cards:　Access, Visa, Amex, Mastercard.
　　　　　Bitters:　Harveys, Pilgrim, 4 guests.
　　　　　 Lagers:　Heineken, Heineken Export, Carling, Tennants Extra, Stella Artois, McEwans LA.

Examples of bar meals (lunch & evening, 7 days): *indoor barbecue, fillet steak with snails, chicken en croute, beef Bellington, spare ribs, steak & kidney pie, Guinness pie, plaice filled with crab & fresh prawns, roast supreme of duck poached in blackberries & apple kaffif, veg curry/lasagne. Trad. Sun. roasts.*

"Always worth a call" is the pub motto, and indeed it's probably best to call ahead if you want to reserve a table, for this is very well frequented establishment, used by the many "celebrities" who live in this salubrious area. Built in the 17th century of ships timbers, it has a single L-shaped bar with indoor barbecue, and there's also a barbecue in the beer garden, which straddles a public footpath leading into the heart of Surrey. Any of the paintings for sale in the bar might make a suitable gift. There's always a friendly atmosphere, especially warm when the log fire is on the go. Of further interest is the duckpond and windmill nearby (the oldest working mill in England). Star rating in leading good pub guide.

THE CRICKETERS ARMS

Stane Street, Ockley, nr Docking   Tel. (0306) 627205

    Location: On A29 south of village centre. Credit cards: Not accepted.
      Bitters: Ringwood Best, Fullers London Pride, Pilgrims Progress, John Smith.
      Lagers: Carlsberg, Fosters.

Examples of bar meals (lunch & evening, 7 days): *deep fried mushrooms & dip, whitebait, prawn cocktail, pate; steaks, mixed grill, pork chop, quarter chicken, gammon, scampi, filed jacket potatoes, salads, ploughman's, sandwiches, daily specials. Selection of sweets. Trad. Sun. roasts.*

The Cricketers embodies all the characteristics of a traditional English country pub. These might be said to comprise three principal factors: the building itself, food and drink, hospitality and atmosphere. On the first count, the pub was built in 1450 - a good age by any standards - and is reportedly home to Victor, a friendly ghost. The inglenook is truly outstanding, and still has the racks used for smoking meals - pigs are roasted over the fire on occasion. The flagstoned floors in the bar area are original, and the timber beams look as though they might be too. Food is straightforward and wholesome, served in generous portions. A welcoming atmosphere is generated in part by the pub itself but mostly by the Francis family, landlords for four years. They welcome children and keep lovely gardens (with pond); flowers and hanging baskets are a delight in summer.

THE CROWN INN

Chiddingfold   Tel. (0428 79) 2255/6
       Location: On A283. Credit cards: Access, Visa, Diners, Amex.
Accommodation: 1 single, 5 doubles, 2 twins, all with full facilities. 3 rooms have 4-posters.
        Bitters: Badger, Tanglefoot, guests.
        Lagers: Hofbrau, guests.

Examples of bar meals (lunch & evening, 7 days): *beef rissoles, steak & kidney pie, spicy chicken, mixed seafood crepes, hot & sour veg & nuts.*
Examples of restaurant meals (lunch & evening except Mons): *feuillette of asparagus & broccoli, fillet of salmon trout on watercress & lime fondue, fillet steak with oysters, breast of chicken stuffed with prawns & cooked in lobster & vermouth sauce, chateaubriand . Trad. Sun. roasts.*

One of the finest examples of a medieval (1258) timber building in the country, The Crown inspires awe in visitors from the New World. They step inside to be confronted by superb linenfold panelling, leaded glass windows, ornate ceilings and enormous fireplaces - fit for royalty, including Edward VI and Elizabeth I who stayed here. Coins dating from the latter's reign were found during building work some years ago. In such surrounds it is almost as a bonus that the food is also first class, whether a la carte in the restaurant or buffet style in the Huntsman Bar. A marvellous venue for a wedding reception, and also to stay, being close to London etc, yet in lovely countryside. Children welcome. Barbecues in small garden Sunday lunchtimes in summer.

THE PRINCE OF WALES

Shere, nr Guildford.   Tel. (048 641) 2313

- Location: Just beyond village square, 1/2 mile off A25.
- Credit cards: Not accepted.
- Bitters: Youngs Ordinary, Special, Extra Light LA.
- Lagers: Youngs London & Premium, Castlemaine, Labatts.

Examples of bar meals (every lunchtime, evenings Wed - Sat, plus Sundays in summer): *fresh local trout, homemade steak & kidney pie, chicken & mushroom pie, curries, scampi, plaice, cod, vegetarian lasagne, salads, ploughman's, sandwiches, daily specials. Banana split, apple pie.*

"The most beautiful village in Surrey" - an assertion commonly heard but rarely disputed. The river Tillingbourne (famed for trout) glides through the heart of Shere, wonderfully peaceful except for the raucous squabbling of ducks, themselves an attraction. This idyll would be incomplete without the friendly local, and the 19th century Prince of Wales amply fulfills the role. Landlord Bob Lintill, who's been here 14 years, is a mine of information about the locale, and will readily tell a few tales, including that of the legend of the 'silent pool'. Wife Kathy prepares generous portions of good food at reasonable prices. Sunday evening in winter is quiz night, and there's occasional live entertainment, but darts, pool and crib are always to hand. Children and dogs are welcome, and there's a garden with barbecue.

THE CRICKETERS

Downside, Cobham. Tel. (0932) 862105
 Fax (0932) 868186
Location: 2 miles south of Cobham on East Horsley road. Credit cards: Access, Visa, Diners, Amex.
Bitters: Ruddles County & Best, Websters.
Lagers: Carlsberg, Fosters, Holstein, Budweiser.

Examples of bar meals (lunch & evening, 7 days): *buffet bar & salads, variety of raised pies, tandoori chicken, veal marsala, gammon , trout with almonds, lamb chop, lasagne, daily specials.*
Examples of restaurant meals (lunch & evening, Tues - Sun lunch): *deep fried cambazola & cranberry sauce, mango & prawn with coronation sauce, veal tropicana, honey glazed rack of lamb, tournedos rossini, Dover sole Waleska with lobster & cream, vegetable koulibiac. Also table d'hote menu with daily specials.*

If you hadn't planned to eat, a glimpse of the buffet bar, arrayed with a wide range of salads and fish and meat selections, is likely to change your mind. Alternatively, the table d'hote menu, very popular with business people, offers a choice of good, hot traditional food. Indeed, this is a place where the best traditions of the English country inn are well observed; standing on the village common and with a lovely garden, the fact that it is over 300 years old is evident from the wattle and daub walls, still visible in parts. Low beamed ceilings, beautiful brickwork, open fireplace and cosy alcoves all make their contribution, but Brian and Wendy Luxford and staff create the friendly atmosphere. Children are allowed in the Stable Bar, there's also a separate restaurant with exceptionally good wine list, and all just 10 minutes from junction 10 of the M25!

THE THAMES COURT

Shepperton Lock, The Towpath, Shepperton.   Tel. (0932) 221957
 Location: From church square take Chertsey road, left into Ferry Lane.
 Credit cards: Access, Visa, Amex.
 Bitters: Bass, IPA, Wadworth 6X, Fullers London Pride.
 Lagers: Carling, Tennants, Tennants Extra, Warsteiner.

Examples of bar/restaurant meals (12 to 8:30pm daily. Afternoon teas 3:30 to 5:30pm): *steak & kidney pie, shepherds pie, Mexican chicken, beef stroganoff, coq au vin, lasagne, honeybaked gammon, roast duck, fresh poached salmon, carvery, jacket potatoes, vegetarian dishes, daily specials. Cold buffet. Trad. Sun. roasts.*

The Dutch ambassador was once the fortunate occupier of this handsome waterside pub, subsequently an exclusive club. It stills looks every inch suited to be the home of a dignitary, beautifully constructed and furnished, and in a marvellous position on the Thames next to busy Shepperton Lock (once classed as Middlesex, but now in Surrey). The main bar is oak panelled and beamed, with a staircase leading to a gallery fitted out in high back seating and private alcoves. The restaurant area (ideal for wedding receptions etc) enjoys lovely views over the water. Food is served buffet style, so there is not a long wait, even when busy - which it usually is, especially on summer days and evenings. Fortunately the garden is large (and has a marquee). Children have rooms set aside away from the bar. Peter Langrish-Smith is your host. Ample parking.

THE CASTLE INN

222 Brox Road, Ottershaw.   Tel. (0932) 872373
        Location: Just off A320, $^1/_2$ mile from junction 11 of M25.
   Credit cards: Not accepted.
         Bitters: Wadworth 6X, Fullers London Pride, Tetley, Burton, guests.
         Lagers: Lowenbrau, Castlemaine, Skol. Addlestones cider.

Examples of bar meals (lunchtimes Mon - Sat, evenings Sat & Sun): *chicken asparagus, best end of lamb, chilli, lasagne, shepherds pie, curry, steak & kidney pie, steaks, fresh skate wings, seafood pancake, cod leek & mushroom pie, cheese & potato pie, savoury macaroni cheese, hazelnut burger with asparagus or almond sauce, quiche, salads, ploughman's, daily specials.*

In just 12 months licensees John and June have transformed their 18th-century inn into one of the best respected in the area. John is a qualified chef and both have considerable experience in the trade. They introduced a greatly enhanced menu, both in respect of quality and variety, but have kept prices remarkably reasonable. Good value, coupled with fine real ales and an authentic 'old world' atmosphere, has brought ever increasing popularity, even in the depths of recession. In the depths of winter the magnificent log fire brings warmth and good cheer, and an interesting collection of antiques and bric-a-brac also lends character. Both bars are very comfortable, with a full quota of exposed brickwork and timbers. In summer the garden and patio are a colourful delight, as is the rose-covered arbour.

THE CRICKETERS

160 Windsor Road, Burrowhill, Chobham. Tel. (0276) 858304
Location: On B383 at northern edge of Chobham, 2 miles off A30.
Credit cards: Access, Visa, Mastercard.
Bitters: Morlands Original, Old Masters, Old Speckled Hen, Everards Tiger.
Lagers: Stella Artois, Hofmeister, Fosters.

Examples from lunch menu (7 days): *Scotch rump, gammon & pineapple, homemade pies (eg steak, kidney & Guinness), chilli, curry, live r & bacon, vegetarian dishes, daily specials.*
Examples from evening menu (except Sun): *deep fried mussels, steaks, chicken Kiev, mixed grill, veal marsala, chicken in orange & ginger, brochette of monkfish with king prawns, grilled Dover sole. Trad. Sun. lunches.*

Landlord (for nine years) Bob Ayres is an exceptionally cordial host, and he seems to have infected his staff, and indeed the pub itself, with good-natured bonhomie. It is the first choice of a loyal band of local regulars, but the newcomer is always warmly greeted and need never feel out of place. A product of the 18th century, the bar lives up to the best English traditions - open log fire, exposed timbers and brickwork (but no jukebox etc) - and in one corner is another icon of an age now past: an old GPO telephone kiosk. Food is homecooked and first rate, yet always reasonably priced. It is best enjoyed in the very pleasant 24-seater restaurant, where children are permitted. There's also a patio and barbecues are held in summer. Car park. Close to Wentworth, Sunningdale and Ascot.

Surrey

THE WHITE HART

47 Guildford Road, Bagshot   Tel. (0276) 473640

    Location: Junction 3 off M3 towards Bracknell, left at lights, right at roundabout. Credit cards: Visa, Mastercard, Eurocard.
    Bitters: Courage Best & Directors, John Smiths, guest.
    Lagers: Hofmeister, Kronenbourg, Fosters, Miller Pilsner.

Examples of bar meals (lunch & evening 7 days, except Sun. evening; available 12 - 9pm Saturdays): *steak & kidney pie, chicken Kiev, chilli (speciality), mixed grill, steak au poivre, plaice, filled jacket potatoes, jumbo sausage & onions, salads, sandwiches, daily specials. Apricot crumble, choc. fudge cake. Children's menu. Trad. Sun. roasts.* NB All-day opening.

The chillis are decidedly not for the faint-hearted, being fearsomely hot and renowned in the area, but steaks and mixed grills are equally celebrated without the attendant risks! All the food is of the first quality and very reasonably priced; Dan and Lyn Jones have, over eight years or so, established a fine reputation for value and friendly efficiency. The pub itself is of uncertain age, but is sufficiently eyecatching to have tempted the Luftwaffe to try and flatten it in World War II. Fortunately they were unsuccessful, and today one finds an L-shaped bar, carpeted and beamed, with stucco walls, soft lighting and well upholstered seating. Children are spoiled with a television in the family room and two aviaries, a fishpond and play equipment in the garden. Once discovered, this is a pub to which you will wish to return. Handy for M3, Ascot and Windsor. Darts.

THE LAMB

593 London Road, Blackwater, nr Camberley   Tel. (0276) 33832
          Location: ½ mile from Camberley town centre on A30.
       Credit cards: Access, Visa, Amex.
            Bitters: Morlands Best, Old Masters, Speckled Hen, Wells Bombardier.
            Lagers: Hofmeister, Stella Artois, Fosters.

Examples of bar meals (lunchtime daily, evenings Tues - Sat.): *chicken Kiev, chilli, steak & kidney pie, mixed grill, scampi, omelettes, salads, ploughman's, sandwiches, daily specials.*
Examples of restaurant meals (as above): *Barnsley chops with port & kidneys, breast of chicken marinated in liqueur served with tangy lemon sauce, beef stroganoff. Sunday lunch carvery.*

Although situated on the junction of the A30 and A321 (one of the busiest in the region), The Lamb is an oasis of peace and good cheer. In their short time as licensees Trevor and Debbie an amicable couple, have wasted no time in making big improvements. The imaginative menu, very keenly priced, is attracting an ever growing clientele. Like the menu, the building itself, dating from the late 19th century, is a successful blend of the old and new. The recently refurbished interior comprises of an L-shaped bar with partially flagstoned floor, a carpeted lounge and well-furnished 24-seater restaurant. A live duo performs regularly. Children are welcome, and the garden has a patio with barbecues planned for the summer of 1993. Ample parking.

THE BAT & BALL

Bat & Ball Lane, Bounstone, Farnham   Tel: (0252) 792108

     Location: 2 miles south of Farnham, off Upper Bourne Lane, Sandrock Hill
 Credit Cards: Access, Visa
      Bitters: Brakspear, Fullers London Pride, Boddingtons, Youngs, guests
       Lagers: Stella Artois, Heineken Export, Budweiser

Examples of bar/restaurant meals (lunch & evening except Sunday evening): *homemade steak & kidney pudding, Thai pork curry, Louisiana jambalaya, fresh game, fresh fish, steaks, beef in wine with walnuts, Caribbean lamb with apricots & coconut, Spanish pork with olives, Lancashire hotpot, Normandy pork, taco stir-fry, vegetarian dishes, filled jacket potatoes, sandwiches, daily specials. Spotted dick, treacle pudding. Children's menu. Trad. Sunday roasts.*

With ever more 'theme pubs' blighting the landscape it is heartening to report that there are still establishments such as this one which seek to cater for all age groups. No purple fluorescent lights or video jukeboxes assault the senses here; instead one has an excellent choice of seven real ales, a wide-ranging menu listing the exotic as well as the traditional (but all home-cooked), and a large, well-furnished family room overlooking the garden with children's play area and barbecue. Karen and Andy, licensees since the summer of 1991, extend cordial greetings to visitors to their 18th-century pub, its many period features including a lovely old fireplace. The elegant 26-seater dining room is noticeably calm and relaxing, but one may also eat in the bar. Crib and dominoes are civilised pastimes, and there's occasional live entertainment. Bird World and Frensham Ponds not far. Rated by national guides.

THE BARLEY MOW

Tilford Green, Tilford, nr Farnham.   Tel. (0252) 792205
  Location: Village green, just off B3001.
  Credit cards: Not accepted.
  Bitters: Courage Directors & Best, John Smiths, guest.
  Lagers: Kronenbourg, Fosters, Carlton LA.

Examples from lunchtime menu (7 days): *homemade steak & kidney pie, fisherman pie, lasagne, homecured ham, plaice, scampi, vegetable lasagne, ploughman's, sandwiches. Apricot crumble, chocolate fudgecake, local farm dairy icecreams. Children's menu.* Examples from evening menu (Mon - Sat): *leek & potato soup, homemade casseroles, fish dishes, chicken Kiev, steaks, jambalaya, moussaka, Florida chicken casserole, vegetarian dishes.*

"Silver" Billy Beldham, famous Surrey and England cricketer, was the first landlord here - his "presence" is still felt sometimes. The green on which this riverside pub has stood since the 1730's is the second oldest cricket ground in the country and, with heartening continuity, the game is still played there. Also unchanging is the wonderfully atmospheric and smokey old bar, with three open fires, one of which is in the separate dining area. Naturally, cricketing pictures adorn the walls, but indoor sportsmen have darts, table skittles and dominoes - and no jukebox! Landlady Penny Bates is a qualified chef, and she and husband George have, over five years, extended a warm welcome to their idyllic country pub, in a lovely setting often used by film makers. Children not permitted inside, but there is a garden (barbecues every Sunday in season). The famous Tilford Oak (in Domesday) and medieval bridge are very near.

THE MARINERS HOTEL

Millbridge, Frensham.   Tel. (025 12) 4747/2050

        Location: On A287, halfway between Farnham and Hindhead.
    Credit cards: Access, Visa, Mastercard, Eurocard, Amex.
  Accommodation: 6 singles, 6 doubles, 8 twins, 1 family. All with full facilities. Special weekend breaks.
         Bitters: Websters, Ruddles, Marston's Pedigree, Royal Oak.
          Lagers: Fosters, Carlsberg, Holsten, Kaliber.

Examples of bar/restaurant meals (lunch & evening, 7 days, all day Sun): *homemade soups, deepfried mushrooms with garlic dip, homemade pizzas, steaks with various sauces, self-serve cold meat buffet & salad bar, daily specials. Children's menu. Homemade gateaux. Trad. Sun. roasts.*

You would barely imagine, admiring the view over the lovely Wey Valley, that the hotel is within an hour of central London, Heathrow or Gatwick. This is one of Surrey's most peaceful and beautiful corners, surrounded by National Trust land and many outdoor activities. Being a family run hotel, pride is taken in the relaxed informality combined with professional service. A fine example of early Victorian architecture, The Mariners is full of character, the timbered bar warmed by log fires, and the opulent restaurant (with dance floor) commanding superb views. Pizzas and pastas are specialities, and the buffet is very popular. Children are welcome, and can play in the garden (with two patios). Quality accommodation and excellent facilities for business meetings/conferences, wedding receptions etc. Live music Monday evenings.

Surrey

THE HOLLY BUSH

Shortfield Common, Frensham.   Tel. (0252) 793593
          Location: Village centre, ½ mile off A287 in direction of Dockenfield.
       Credit cards: Access, Visa.
            Bitters: Morlands Old Master & Old Speckled Hen, Chas Wells Bombardier, guest.
             Lagers: Stella Artois, Fosters, Hofmeister.

Examples of bar meals (lunch & evening, except Sun evening): *h/m steak & kidney pie, cottage pie, chilli, steak, lasagne, scampi, plaice, cod, vegetable lasagne, filled jacket potatoes, ploughman's, sandwiches, daily specials eg liver & bacon, chicken cacciatora. Apple pie, pecan pie, chocolate fudgecake.*
Examples of restaurant meals (evenings only): *veal escalope, steaks, lamb cutlets Shrewsbury, chicken Kiev, trout meuniere. lemon sole. Meringue glace, banana split.* Trad. Sun roast lunches. Booking advised weekends.

Even with 18 years behind them and a very well established reputation, Simon and Jenny Hitchcock are not ones to let standards slip, and strive hard to maintain excellence. Jenny's cooking is much in demand, so booking is advised at weekends. Simon takes pride in the well-kept ales. Their 19th-century pub stands on the edge of the beautiful old village of Fresham, near Frensham Ponds, 'Bird World' and the Agricultural Museum. The lively Public Bar has darts and a pool table, while the comfortable lounge is rather more sedate and is the main eating area. Worthy of special mention is an interesting display of model cars, vans, buses and the like in a showcase. Children are welcome at lunchtimes and the garden has play equipment. Car park.

THE PHOENIX INN

London Road, Hartley Wintney, nr Basingstoke.   Tel. (0252) 842484
      Location: On A30 1 mile west of village (next to Texaco garage).
  Credit cards: Access, Visa, Diners, Amex.
       Bitters: Friary, Old Dray, Burton, Youngs Special.
       Lagers: Lowenbrau, Skol, Castlemaine.

Examples of bar meals (lunch & evening except Sun. evening): *potted shrimps, smoked mackerel, pan-fried steaks, gammon, scampi, plaice, salads, ploughman's, sandwiches, daily specials. Range of sweets.*
Examples of restaurant meals (evenings except Sun.): *all of above, hot king prawns, fillet steak au poivre, Scotch smoked salmon, pork chop. Trad. Sun. lunch: 2 roasts & pie/pudding alternative.*

The eponymous mythical bird appeared on the coat of arms of a lady friend of Henry VIII, so the story goes, and the inn was built by him as a 'grace and favour' house. Whether or not this is true, there is no doubting the antiquity of the low beams in the lounge bar. This overlooks the large, secluded garden and patio, and also leads to the 25-seater restaurant with attractive brick fireplace.
The front bar has darts, shove ha'penny and crib. Landlord Bob Coleman has, over 17 years (an exceptionally long tenure these days), established a large and loyal local following. Customers are happy to travel a good distance for well-prepared food (microwave strictly taboo), the period atmosphere and the geniality of Bob and his staff. Children welcome inside on Sundays. Barbecues planned for summer.

Hampshire

THE OLD HOUSE AT HOME

Tylney Lane, Newnham Green, Newnham, nr Hook.   Tel. (0256) 762222
       Location: On village green.
    Credit cards: Access, Visa.
         Bitters: Ushers Founders & Best, Bensons Old Sox, Courage Best.
          Lagers: Budweiser, Kronenbourg, Fosters, Holsten Export.

Examples of bar/restaurant meals (lunch & evening, 7 days): *famous sausage menu (eg Creole jazz, Greek, Cajun, Welsh leek), marinated lamb steak, breast of duck in black cherry sauce, chicken tikka masala, steaks, lasagne, lemon sole, salmon en croute, daily speci als. Spotted dick, treacle pudding, Mississippi mud pie, lemon lush. Trad. Sun. roasts.*

'Banger' is decidedly not a word one would use here; the exotic range of sausages (12 on a separate menu) is made to the very highest standards, using only the leanest cuts of meat and freshly blended seasoning - monosodium glutamate and preservatives are strictly taboo. Many of the recipes are centuries old, and great care goes into the preparation - a truly unique gastronomic experience, and there are plenty of tasty alternatives, all good value. Edward and Loretta like to live up to the pub's name, and the atmosphere is always homely and welcoming. The situation on the village green is also most agreeable. Children are welcome in the eating area and barbecues are held in the garden in summer. The Barn Restaurant doubles as a function room. Darts. Car park.

THE CROOKED BILLET

London Road, Hook.   Tel. (0256) 762118
       Location: On A30, ½ mile east of Hook.
    Credit cards: Not accepted.
        Bitters: Courage Directors & Best (& dark mild), John Smiths.
        Lagers: Fosters, Kronenbourg, Hofmeister.

Examples of bar meals (lunch & evening, 7 days): *butterfly prawns, giant Yorkshire puddings, gammon steak, prime Scottish steaks, scampi, h/m seafood pasta, moussaka, curries, deep fried chicken fillets, vegetable lasagne, salads, ploughman's, sandwiches, daily specials. Tennessee grasshopper pie, hot Alabama fudge cake, apple pie, icecreams & sorbets.*

A billet is a piece of wood, designed to tell travellers that here is a place of rest and refreshment. It is indeed singularly restful to sit by a river, and the Whitewater (full of trout) runs through the pleasant garden, a quiet refuge from the busy A30. Refreshment comes in the form of an excellent range of beers, and a wide choice of mostly homecooked food, supplemented further on special nights. Richard and Sally Sanders are friendly young hosts; they've been here since September '86 and oversaw full refurbishment in '88. Two log fires and an 'old world' bar belie the true age of the building; it dates from 1934, yet has already managed to accumulate a crop of ghost stories. The spacious eating area is nicely furnished with velvet drapes and carpeted throughout. Children and dogs on leads are welcome. Ample parking.

Hampshire

THE SWAN

Hook Road, North Warnborough, nr Odiham.   Tel. (0256) 702727
- Location: On A32 1½ miles from junction 5 of M3.
- Credit cards: Access, Visa, Amex, Switch.
- Bitters: Courage Directors & Best, Wadworth 6X, Marstons Pedigree, John Smiths
- Lagers: Kronenbourg, Fosters, Carlsberg. Scrumpy Jack & Strongbow cider.

Examples of bar meals (lunch & evening, 7 days): *lamb samosas, char-grills, curries, chilli, sweet & sour pork, chicken briev, cottage pie, lemon sole, Scottish salmon, nut cutlet Wellington, jacket potatoes, sandwiches, daily specials. Death by chocolate, hot butterscotch & walnut flan, spotted dick, raspberry royale. Trad. Sun. roast £5.85.*

Charles I reputedly hid here from marauding Roundheads. It's quite conceivable, as parts of the building were 300 years old even then, and no doubt full of concealed nooks and crannies. These days the atmosphere is notably more relaxed and congenial. Landlord Simon Windle acquired the licence only recently, but was manager and chef for the previous three years. Aided by amicable staff he is building successful trade at this peaceful country pub. 'Olde Worlde' it certainly is, replete with original timbers and a magnificent inglenook in the lounge. This overlooks a beautifully laid out patio and garden (with playground), shaded by trees and wonderfully tranquil. The sizable menu incorporates a blend of old English favourites with well established 'imports' like chilli, chicken tikka or lasagne. Children welcome. Darts, dominoes, crib.

THE FOX

Green Lane, Ellisfield, nr Basingstoke   Tel. (0256) 381210

      Location: 3 miles off A339 via B3046, southern edge of village.
  Credit cards: Access, Visa, Mastercard, Eurocard.
       Bitters: Marstons Pedigree, Wadworth 6X, Gales HSB, Fullers London Pride, Theakstons Old Peculier, King Alfred's Hampshire, Tanglefoot.
        Lagers: McEwans, Becks.

Examples of bar meals (lunch & evening, except Mon evening): steaks, Scotch salmon, rainbow trout, lamb in mint casserole, vegetarian dishes, filled jacket potatoes, salads, ploughman's, sandwiches, daily specials eg casseroles.

In the lovely rolling countryside of the North Downs, The Fox is about as remote as you can be in Hampshire, yet people travel some distance to seek it out. Word has spread of the very good food and exceptional range of quality ales, not overlooked either by Egon Ronay and Camra guides, and indeed often recommended by other publicans! Few come only once, most return again and again, for licensees (of five years) Ray and Glenys strive to make sure that their guests always enjoy their visit. One may partake of their homecooked fare in either bar. 16th century in origin, the main lounge is split level, with exposed beams, open fireplace, comfortable seating and an attractive bay window. Darts are played in the public bar, where dogs are permitted. Children are allowed only in the rather nice garden. Car parking.

Hampshire

THE STAR INN

London Road, Bentley, nr Farnham.   Tel. (0420) 23184
        Location: Village centre, mid-way between Farnham and Alton.
     Credit cards: Visa, Mastercard.
          Bitters: Courage Best, Ushers Best, Founders, Triple Crown.
          Lagers: Fosters, Kronenbourg, Miller Pilsner.

Examples of bar/dining room meals (lunchtime daily, evenings Tues - Sat): *steaks, beef stroganoff, lemon chicken & tarragon, Barnsley chop, Somerset pork, curry, moussaka, coachman's pie, salmon & prawn gratin, grilled halibut, cod, scampi, vegetable mornay, salads, ploughman's, sandwiches, daily specials. Good range of sweets. Trad. Sun. roasts.*

Listeners to Radio 4's serial 'The Village', set in Bentley, will know of The Star as the focal point of village life. That is no fiction: this cheerful Victorian pub draws custom from many miles around. Trevor (former Environmental Health Officer) and Ann Cooper (both from Farnham) have, over four years or so, built a first rate reputation for good, wholesome food at very fair prices. Although the outward aspect of the building is not the most striking you will see in this area, inside is bright and welcoming, the decor not overly ornate. The single bar, divided into two sections, is carpeted and oak-panelled, but the dining room (children welcome) is especially attractive, with polished walnut tables and tasteful pictures and plates. There is no garden, and the car park is sited opposite the pub.

Hampshire

THE GREYFRIAR

Winchester Road, Chawton, nr Alton.　　　　　　　　Tel. (0420) 83841
　　　Location:　Village centre, opposite Jane Austen's House.
　　Credit cards:　Access, Visa, Mastercard, Eurocard.
　　　　Bitters:　Wadworth 6X, Strongs Country, Flowers Original, Brakspear.
　　　　Lagers:　Heineken Export, Stella Artois, Fosters.

Examples of bar meals (lunch & evening, except Sun. evenings): *beefsteak & kidney pie, braised lambs liver & onions, fish platter, jacket potatoes, salads, sandwiches, club special, ploughman's, vegetarian lasagne, daily specials.*
Examples of restaurant meals (as above): *baked trout with prawns & lemon butter, half roast duckling with orange sauce, steaks, daily specials eg lobster thermidor, roast loin of pork. Trad. Sun. roasts.*

Jane Austen spent her last eight years of life in this pleasant little village (dating from Saxon times and mentioned in Domesday), penning some of her most successful novels, including 'Pride and Prejudice' and 'Sense and Sensibility'. Her former house is open to the public, an important tourist draw. Some landlords would be tempted to cash in on this, but Shirley and Ken Balfour (licensees since 1990) have made their early 16th-century pub popular with locals and visitors for good food at very reasonable prices. They have also refurbished to a high standard, carefully preserving period charm. An upstairs room accommodates up to 25 for a private function. Weather permitting, barbecues are held Sunday evenings, and there's also live entertainment on Sundays. Children are welcome, and there's a play area plus garden and patio. Darts. Ample parking.

Hampshire

THE SWAN HOTEL

11 West Street, Alresford Tel. (0962) 732302

  Location: Village centre.
  Credit cards: Access, Visa, Switch.
  Accommodation: 19 doubles, 4 twins. All en suite, T.V., direct 'phone, tea tray, newspaper. De luxe rooms have hair-dryer, trouser press. From £32.50 single, £40 double, £47.50 family incl.
  Bitters: Courage Best, John Smith.
  Lagers: Fosters, Kronenbourg.

Examples of bar meals (lunch & evening, 7 days): *homemade curries, beef in Guinness, chilli liver & onions, steak & kidney pie, lasagne, fresh grilled sardines, trout, vegetarian pasta bake, salads, ploughman's, sandwiches. Children's menu.*
Examples of restaurant meals (evening, 7 days): *crispy roasted duckling, fresh herb pancake, fresh local trout, steak Dianne, chicken Kiev, nachos, veal in creamy stilon & mushroom sauce. Trad. Sun. roasts £7.95. Bar menus also available. Afternoon teas from 3 to 6pm.*

This is one of those fine old coaching inns which grace many of our small towns and, like most of the better ones, is family-run. Under the stewardship of the Warwick family for 13 years, currently managed by daughter Angela Graham (cousin to racing driver Derek Warwick), the hotel dates from 1552 at the latest. Perhaps the most illustrious visitor amongst many was Oliver Cromwell, hence the Cromwell's Bar, a remarkable room to be found in the crypt, accommodating 120 and suitable for functions. Duets or trios perform live on Saturday evenings. Darts in main bar. Children welcome. Bedrooms exceptionally well appointed. Alresford Steam Railway 200 yards away.

THE BUSH INN

Ovington, nr Alresford.　　　　　　　　　　Tel. (0962) 732764
　　　　Location:　In village by river Itchen, ½ mile off A31.
　　Credit cards:　Visa, Mastercard.
　　　　　Bitters:　Wadworth 6X, Flowers Original, Gales HSB, Strongs Country.
　　　　　Lagers:　Stella Artois, Heineken.

Examples of bar meals (lunch & evening, 7 days): *grilled Itchen trout, homemade chilli, green lipped mussels in garlic butter, scampi, sirloin steak, cold fish platter, salads, ploughman's, sandwiches, daily specials eg venison & duck ragout, grilled salmon. Children's lunches. Good range of sweets.*
Examples of restaurant meals (lunch & evening, except Sun evening): *spinach & vegetable roulade, Bush Inn fillet (wrapped in bacon, stuffed with stilton), rack of lamb, escalopes of venison, honey-glazed duck breast. Strawberry & almond layer shortbread, sticky toffee pudding, banana fritters. Trad. Sun. roasts.*

Derived, appropriately, from the Latin for 'resting place', The Bush stands on the Pilgrim's Way, and has provided rest and refreshment to the weary traveller since the 17th century. And what an idyllic spot to do so, with lovely riverside walks and beautiful shaded garden - film-makers know the spot well. The inn itself is a well suited for quiet repose: no juke boxes etc, but fires in every room, old timbers, clocks and furniture, and many brasses, coppers and antiques. Service is friendly and efficient, and the menus are very diverse and imaginative, both in bar and high class 30-seater restaurant, as the examples above indicate. Under the new owner ship of Geoff and Sue Draper, The Bush remains quite memorable, well worth taking a little trouble to find.

Hampshire

THE PLOUGH INN

East Stratton, nr Winchester.   Tel. (0962) 774241
Location: ½ mile off A33.
Credit cards: Not accepted.
Accommodation: 1 double en suite (£42.50), 3 twins (£37.50). Tv's, tea & coffee.
Bitters: Butser Brew, HSB, Ringwood 49.
Lagers: Carlsberg, Tennents Extra, Carling.

Examples of bar meals (lunch & evening, Tues - Sun): *beef curry, Gambas prawns in garlic butter, chilli, rumpsteak (evenings only), homemade burgers (evenings only), ploughman's, sandwiches, daily specials eg rabbit casserole. Whisky bread pudding with whisky sauce, rhubarb tart.*
Examples of restaurant meals (evenings Wed - Sun): *homemade soups (noted), braised pigeon, jugged hare, game casserole, steaks, beef in Guinness, fillets of plaice stuffed with seafood, salmon steak. Trad. Sun. lunches.*

Country pursuits are a theme at this 19th century former bakery, in a lovely thatched village (mentioned in Domesday). Those fond of hare, pheasant, partridge et al will find much to please them, but there are plenty of alternatives, all prepared by landlady (for six years) Trudy Duke, whose soups enjoy a special reputation. Son Richard is the sportsman, and charming old pictures of game birds and country scenes grace the dining room (known as the 'game room') and two bars, both warmed by open fires. The lounge is quiet and restful, the public has darts, and is where the locals gather. A skittle alley doubles as a function room, and there's live music on occasion. Children are welcome, and a tractor is amongst the play equipment on the large green at the front.

THE QUEEN INN

Down Street, Dummer, nr Basingstoke.   Tel. (0256) 397367

    Location: Village centre, ½ mile from jnctn 7 of M3.
  Credit cards: Access, Visa, Amex, Switch.
      Bitters: Courage Best, Directors, Fullers London Pride.
      Lagers: Kronenbourg, Hofmeister, Fosters.

Examples of bar/restaurant meals (lunch & evening, except Sun evening): *kidney turbigo, sausage confit, large avocado & prawns salad , 10ozs rib eye steak, deep pan lasagne, Chinese sweet & sour chicken, chilli, whole plaice, sandwiches, jacket potatoes, ploughman's, daily specials. Homemade cheesecake, chocolate mousse, fruit pie. Trad. 4-course Sun. lunch £8.95.*

A portrait of our queen hangs on a wall in this esteemed village pub, but we lesser mortals are equally assured of a genuine welcome from John and Jocelyn Holland, who've 'reigned' for over nine years. Their well-timbered 17th century pub has just the one, L-shaped bar, warmed by a large open fire, but also has a dining area (children welcome) which seats 30 and four other sections where bar food may be consumed. That is except for Sunday evenings, which is set aside for live music. Bar billiards is another entertainment. Fresh flowers add their inimitable touch to a very attractive interior, and outside is a safe, enclosed garden and patio with tables and chairs - ask about barbecues. Wayfarer Walk and Micheldever Forest nearby. Car park.

Hampshire

THE WATERSHIP DOWN INN

Freefolk Priors, Freefolk, nr Whitchurch   Tel. (0256) 892254
     Location: Just off B3400 between Whitchurch and Overton.
   Credit cards: Not accepted.
      Bitters: Hampshire, Archers, Greene King, Ringwood, Youngs, Brakspear.
      Lagers: Becks, Carlsberg Export, Castlemaine.

Examples of bar meals (lunch & evening except Sun. evening & all day Mon.): *homemade cottage pie, lemony chicken, chilli, steak & kidney pie, chicken & mushroom pie, steaks, trout, scampi, pork vindaloo, vegetarian tagliatelle, filled jacket potatoes, ploughman's, sandwiches, daily specials. Trad. Sun. roasts (to order) in winter only.*

It would be almost sacrilege to put rabbit on the menu when one is so close to that rodent Mecca, Watership Down. Author Richard Adams lives locally, and his story is centred around the River Test, the railway line (both within 100 yards of the pub) and the beautiful surrounding countryside. Those quite unmoved by the plight of hapless bunnies will still find much to please them at this agreeable timbered 19th-century pub. The landlord and his family are most welcoming, the food is good and exceptional value-for-money. There is a separate dining room, but in summer most of the eating is done in the large garden, which has barbecue and play equipment. Live music is heard monthly, quiz and crib nights weekly. Large car park.

Hampshire

THE GEORGE & DRAGON

Townsend, Wolverton, nr Basingstoke. Tel. (0635) 298292

- Location: 1 mile off A339 between Newbury and Basingstoke (turn at sign to Townsend, Baughurst, Wolverton & Stony Heath).
- Credit cards: Access, Visa.
- Bitters: Brakspears Special, Wadworth 6X & Henrys IPA, Fullers London Pride, John Smiths, McEwans Export, King Alfred.
- Lagers: Fosters, Kronenbourg, Carlsberg.

Examples of bar meals (lunch & evening, 7 days): *homemade steak & kidney pie, venison pie, chicken curry, chilli, lasagne, steaks, kebabs, scampi, plaice, ploughman's, sandwiches, daily specials eg pheasant pie with Guinness, gammon cooked in dry cider. Homebaked apple & blackberry pie, strawberry gateau.*

Any pub which is a little tricky to find needs to be special, and this 17th-century freehouse is certainly that. Good, homecooked food and an excellent selection of ales are two worthy reasons for a visit, and the reception from Lionel and Paula Shore, an exceptionally amiable couple who've been here since 1985, helps establish a genial atmosphere. Paula is also a very good cook and prepares everything on the premises. In a new building to the rear they have recently constructed a skittle alley and function room. This is quite self-contained, comfortably furnished and carpeted, with a dance floor and room for 70 seated, 130 standing. A superb hot or cold buffet can be laid on. The old coaching inn itself, oak-beamed and with a large inglenook, has darts and bar billiards. Children welcome in function room and garden.

Hampshire

THE GEORGE INN

Vernham Dean, nr Andover.　　　　　　　　　　　Tel. (0264 87) 279

　　　Location:　Village centre, 3 miles off A343.
　Credit cards:　Not accepted.
　　　　Bitters:　Marston's.
　　　　Lagers:　Marston's Pilsner, Stella Artois.

Examples of bar meals (lunch & evening, 7 days): *George Inn mushrooms (garlic flavoured topped with cheese & bacon), homemade soups, corned beef hash pie, ploughman's, many daily specials eg chicken in white wine, cottage pie, bacon & cheese layer pie, 'leeky bakes', liver & bacon, lasagne.*

Close to the Wiltshire and Berkshire borders in wonderful walking country, this picture-book early 17th century inn is immediately likeable. Perhaps it's the tiled roof curving over the windows, or the fairly uncommon timbered brick and flint walls, but on entering one's first impressions are confirmed. Each of the heavily timbered bars has a fireplace, the main bar an inglenook with seating. Furnishings are simple but comfortable, but most important, perhaps, is the good, wholesome, homecooked food, changing daily, plus the esteemed Marston's ales, which have earned a place in major good pub guides. Mary Perry, an amiable landlady ably assisted by husband Philip, is the force behind this; she has spent 23 years running local pubs, the last four at this one. They have a family room and attractive garden. Well controlled dogs and children permitted. Car park.

Hampshire

THE WHITE HART INN

High Street, Stockbridge.　　　　　　　　　　　Tel. (0264) 810663
　　　　　　　　　　　　　　　　　　　　　　　Fax (0264) 810268

<table>
<tr><td>Location:</td><td>At roundabout.</td></tr>
<tr><td>Credit cards:</td><td>Access, Visa, Mastercard.</td></tr>
<tr><td>Accommodation:</td><td>3 singles, 10 doubles (inc. 4-poster), 2 family. Some en suite, all with TV, cntrl htng, tea & coff. From £30 single, £42.50 double. Weekend breaks £70pp, incl. dinner, b & b.</td></tr>
<tr><td>Bitters:</td><td>Wadworth 6X, Bass, Worthington, guest.</td></tr>
<tr><td>Lagers:</td><td>Carling, Tennents.</td></tr>
</table>

Examples of bar meals (lunch & evening, 7 days): *homemade steak & kidney pie, cottage pie topped with cheesy potato, curry, chilli, scampi, fisherman's/ploughman's lunch, salads, sandwiches, daily special.*
Examples of restaurant meals (as above): *prawn pancakes, raspberry avocado; local trout stuffed with apricots, queen scallops sauted with bacon & mushrooms in creamy sauce, guinea fowl in sauce of morello cherries, steaks, vegetable korma. Trad. Sun. roasts £9.75.*

Reputedly the finest trout stream in the world, the Test flows through the village, and many fish find their way to the tables of this outstanding 12th century country inn. If walls could speak, they would tell many a tale; one adjoining the inn is pitted with hollows formed by sharpening swords. Trustees of this long history of innkeeping, the Curtis family have, over 17 years, introduced modern comforts, consistent with the ancient character of the building. The latest addition has been the Walnut Tree Wine Bar (facilities for private and business functions), with a quite different atmosphere to the Shavers Restaurant and live music some evenings. Excellent base to stay, popular with locals and anglers. Garden. Car park. Recommended by major good pub guides.

THE CARTWHEEL INN

Whitsbury, nr Fordingbridge.   Tel. (0725 3) 362

      Location: Village centre.
 Credit cards: Amex, Diners, Visa, Mastercard, Eurocard.
       Bitters: Adnams Broadside, Bass, Theakstons Old Peculier, Marston's Pedigree, Wadworth 6X, McEwans Export, Timothy Taylor's Landlord, Mitchels Mild. Everchanging choice - some 150 p.a.
        Lagers: Carlsberg, Fosters, Heineken, Stella Artois, Becks.

Examples of bar/restaurant meals (lunch & evening, except Tues evening): *Whitsbury-grown garlic mushrooms, homecooked steak & kidney pudding, lasagne, steaks, Cartwheel special potatoes, fresh fish, Poole crabs, swordfish steaks, cashew paella, pasta parmagiana, salads, ploughman's, sandwiches, daily specials. Homemade profiteroles, bread pudding, New Forest icecreams.*

"Slightly off the beaten track, but never in a rut!" - this Cartwheel is the only pub for miles around, but that's not why it is so well used by locals, nor why it is rated by major guides. It's a fine example of an unpretentious working village local, serving an exceptional range of beers and good food. The magnificent Desert Orchid ("Dessie") was stabled in Whitsbury - there is some influence from the stud farm, but one could not describe the inn as 'horsey'. It was once a wheelwright's (hence the name) and back in the 1800's a barn. Momentos from its past make interesting decor. Two main bars, a games room (with pool and darts) and dining room are all imbued with warmth and character - look for the old baking ovens either side of the main fireplace. Ian and Jeanie are young licensees, but have already put in over eight years here. Their garden has play equipment and barbecue, but unfortunately there is no facility for children inside the pub.

THE WOOLPACK INN

Sopley, nr Christchurch.   Tel. (0425) 72252
       Location: Village centre.
    Credit cards: Access, Visa.
        Bitters: Marstons Pedigree, Wadworth 6X, Ringwood Best, Whitbread.
        Lagers: Heineken, Heineken Premier.

Examples of bar meals (lunch & evening, 7 days): *cod in beer batter, steak & Guinness pie, homemade lasagne, barbecue ribs, lamb cut lets in mint gravy, grilled local plaice, braised steak Bordelaise, hock of gammon in honey & cider, vegetable lasagne, ploughperson's lunch, Dutch open rolls. Lemon meringue pie, treacle tart, chocolate fudge cake. Trad. Sun. roasts.*

Fish and chips in newspaper (if requested) is an old English custom, revived here, oddly enough, by Dutch landlord Dick Goematt. 18 years a restaurateur in his native country, he and wife Barbara took over in April 1990, and they and their eager-to-please staff have made this 17th century pub not only very popular, but also recommended by a major national good pub guide. The Union Jack flutters proudly in the garden, and the menu also reflects the best of British, with overseas favourites also well represented. On entering by the back door look up and you will see a lady in the stocks, allegedly a customer who didn't pay or a waitress who didn't smile! There are no ghosts, but an 'invisible pianist' (pianola) provides background music. Children under 14 are not permitted inside, but there's an attractive garden with a stream running through it. Function room for 35.

Hampshire

CHAMPAGNE CHARLIES

45 St Thomas Street, Lymington. Tel. (0590) 672004
Location: Top of High Street.
Credit cards: Access, Visa, Amex.
Bitters: Eldridge Pope Best, Dorchester, Royal Oak, Hardys Country.
Lagers: Faust, Labatts.

Examples of bar meals (lunch & evening, 7 days): *crab thermidor, spicy chicken buffalo wings, daily fish catch (plaice, sole, skate), fisherman's pie, lobster thermidor, steak & kidney pie, hickory smoked ham, moussaka, vegetable lasagne, salads, ploughman's, sandwiches, daily specials eg fresh lobster salad, local mackerel with dill & mustard sauce. Spotted dick, apple pie, gateaux. Trad. Sun . roasts.*

"The Seafood King of Lymington", proclaims landlord Charles Taylor, modestly, and who would argue? Neptune's provenance has only a short trip from trawler to table, so all is absolutely fresh. Although not a formal restaurant, the dining area seats 50 and there is table service - restaurant meals at bar prices. The pub, dating from around 1700, was known as The Lobster Pot when Charles arrived with Jane (now his wife) in early 1988. Actor, bon viveur and friend of Charles, Oliver Reed, gave it its new and appropriate name - Charles is a sparkling and attentive host, but never overwhelming. The maritime theme extends to the decor; the walls are covered with paintings and prints of Cunard liners and, interestingly, menus from those liners. Children welcome, but no garden. Large public car park opposite. Close to Beaulieu, New Forest and Isle of Wight ferry.

THE RED LION

Boldre, Lymington. Tel. (0590) 673177
      Location: Village centre, ¼ mile off A335.
   Credit cards: Access, Visa.
       Bitters: Eldridge Pope Dorchester & Royal Oak, Thomas Hardy County.
      Lagers: Faust, Kronenbourg. Plus Guinness.

Examples of bar meals (lunch & evening, 7 days): *homecooked gammon with poached eggs, half duckling with wine soaked orange slices, scampi, lamb cutlets with rosemary, vegetable casserole topped with cheese, salads, ploughman's, sandwiches. Homemade apple pie, sherry trifle, profiteroles, knickerbocker glory. Menu revised weekly.*

"One cannot judge a book by its cover" - a wise maxim, but in this case what awaits inside lives up to the promise of the pretty exterior. The original cottage is recorded in Domesday as brewing and selling ale, but the inn dates from 1680, and stands on a river crossing by the village green on the edge of the New Forest. Mr and Mrs Bicknell have invested 18 years in making their business successful, the friendly atmosphere, good food and wine having earned a star rating in a major national good pub guide. A multitude of chamber pots festoons the two heavily beamed bars, along with copper pans, harnesses, gin traps and much more. One room was converted from the stable (the original hay racks can still be seen along one wall), and open fires broadcast cheering warmth throughout. Children over 14 welcome. Garden and ample parking. Spinners Garden (noted for rare shrubs) nearby.

Hampshire

THE NEW FOREST INN

Emery Down, Lyndhurst.   Tel. (0703) 282329

        Location: Village centre, ½ mile from A35.
   Credit cards: Access, Visa.
Accommodation: 4 doubles en suite. £25 single, £50 double, incl.
         Bitters: Flowers Original, Strong Country, Wadworth 6X.
          Lagers: Stella Artois, Heineken.

Examples of bar meals (lunch & evening, 7 days): *fillet of pork in green peppercorn sauce, breast of chicken in stilton sauce, veal italian, salmon in champagne, pigeon breast Rufus, garlic & herb pasta, steak. Hot apple & cider pudding, homemade cheesecake.*

There's a story that in the early 1700s beer was sold from a caravan on this site, having claimed squatter's rights, and that caravan now forms the front lounge porchway. Stranger still, the sound of curtains drawn on brass rings can apparently be heard daily at 5pm! Three rooms open off the single servery: the lower bar, which seats 18; the main bar, with private 'bays' (including the body of the caravan); and the lighter upper bar, decorated by old farm implements. Morris dancers perform on occasion, and the Hampshire Youth Orchestra give concerts in the garden, which on a long summer evening here in the heart of the New Forest must be a delight. Children are welcome, and will no doubt head for the ponies in the neighbouring paddock. Sue and Nick Emberley are also proprietors of the Trusty Servant at Minstead and the Fleur de Lys at Pilley, and maintain high standards of good, imaginative food at each.

THE OLD HOUSE AT HOME

Love Lane, Romsey.   Tel. (0794) 513175

    Location: 400 yards east of town centre.
 Credit cards: Not accepted.
     Bitters: Gales Best, HSB.
     Lagers: Tennents Extra, Carling.

Examples of bar meals (lunch & evening, 7 days): *farmhouse pate, baked mushrooms in herb & cheese sauce, big Yorkshire pudding (filled with steak, kidney, mushrooms & vegetables in Guinness gravy), jambalaya, chicken & tomato crunch, prawn fritters, goujons of salmon, steaks & grills, daily specials.*

Examples of restaurant meals (as above): *oriental parcels, salmon en croute, stuffed plaice Dieppe, lemon sole Breton, biriani turkey breast, fillet steak. Trad. Sun. roasts.*

A rare sight in England, the salmon leap as they swim up the River Test, which flows through a nearby park. Some will make the short journey to the kitchens of this very popular 15th century pub, where fresh fish is a speciality. The farmer who built it also brewed beer, and his vats are still there in outbuildings. He would doubtless be pleased to see his investment still put to good use and remaining quite unspoilt, despite necessary renovations and extensions - farmhouse origins are unmistakable in the 20-seater restaurant. Custodians for over 22 years, Barrie and Wendy welcome allcomers, young and old, locals and visitors. About once a month they hold "fun evenings" - could be American (everyone dresses up), for example, plus barbecues in the garden in season. Children welcome. Rated by good pub guides.

Hampshire

THE GEORGE INN

Portsdown Hill, Portsmouth. Tel. (0705) 376756
Location: At junction of Portsdown Hill Road and old A3 at top of hill.
Credit cards: Not accepted.
Bitters: Morlands Old Speckled Hen, Strongs Country, Flowers Original, Marstons Pedigree, Boddingtons.
Lagers: Heineken, Heineken Export, Stella Artois.

Examples of bar meals (lunchtimes only, daily except Sun.): *homemade lasagne, chilli, curry, ploughman's, large baton rolls, daily specials eg cottage pie, beef casserole. Chocolate trufito, icecream.*

"A happy family home, open to the public twice a day" - a refreshingly simple philosophy which harks back to the days when that is exactly what pubs were. They are the words of John and Karen Balsom, whose home this has been for around three years. It stands on an escarpment, commanding splendid views over Portsmouth, the Solent and the Isle of Wight. You may be greeted at the door by the resident black cat, who will escort you to your table and may even elect to join you for a meal (tuna preferred). It is not clear how old the building is, but one clue is a sign above a door saying "Old Widley Fire Station. Do not obstruct", and a nearby hayrack suggests the engine was horse-drawn. Traditional pub games are played (no darts or pool), and there is a carol service and occasional Morris dancing. Straightforward and very inexpensive home cooking is served at lunchtime, the evenings being more for conversation over a pint of well-kept ale. A brick table on the patio houses a time capsule from the Round Table; let us hope whoever opens it in the future will find The George is unchanged.

Hampshire

THE BAT & BALL

Broadhalfpenny Down, Hambledon.　　　　　　　　Tel. (0705) 632692
　　　Location: At crossroads between Hambledon and Clanfield.
　　Credit cards: Access, Visa, Diners, Amex.
　　　　Bitters: Friary Meux, Burtons, John Bull. Ind Coope dark mild.
　　　　Lagers: Castlemaine, Lowenbrau, Skol, Swan Light.

Examples of bar meals (lunch & evening, 7 days): *homemade steak & kidney pie/pudding, cottage pie, chicken & ham pie, lasagne, steaks, curries, roast chicken, plaice, scampi, cheese & onion pie, peanut bake, salads, ploughman's, sandwiches, daily specials.*
Examples of restaurant meals (as above): *steaks, venison in red wine, chicken Maryland, pheasant braised in red wine sauce, beef Wellington, chef's mixed grill, poached salmon with asparagus, lemon sole bonne femme, salads, vegetarian dishes. Trad. Sun. roasts - book two weeks ahead.*

The Bat and Ball occupies a hallowed place in the annals of cricket. From 1770 during the 'Hambledon Era' the club was chief authority in the game, its laws adopted nationally. Many big matches were played on the famous down against All England, and a replica scorecard of an especially heroic victory is one of many memorabilia on display. Having been the pavilion and clubhouse, the pub is a Mecca to devotees of our cherished national sport. But most people who come do so for the high standards of food, service and relaxation - the advice to book at least two weeks ahead for Sunday lunch speaks volumes. Guardians of the 'shrine' are Bill and Jean Galbraith - Bill was Ind Coope Cellarman of 1989 and finalist in 1990. They accept children as 'seen but not heard'. Daytime functions in dining room.

Hampshire

THE HAMPSHIRE BOWMAN

Dundridge, Bishop's Waltham, nr Southampton.   Tel. (0489) 892940
- Location: 1½ miles north east of Bishop's Waltham, 1¼ miles east off B3035.
- Credit cards: Not accepted.
- Accommodation: Camping site for tents and caravans.
- Bitters: King & Barnes, Festive, Sussex, Old Ale (winter), Archers Village & Golden, guest.
- Lagers: Hacker Pschorr (Munich), Fosters.

Examples of bar meals lunch & evening Tues - Sat, plus Sun lunch): *garlic & herb king prawns, lemon sole, lasagne, sirloin steak, kaeng hunglay (mild Thai curry), homebaked ham, vegetarian dishes, ploughman's, sandwiches. Children's menu.*

Tucked away down a single-track country lane in the Hampshire downlands, this unpretentious 19th century freehouse (originally known as The Jubilee) is ideal for walkers and is also a pleasant drive for the less energetic. The one small bar room is warmed from two open fires. The walls are bedecked with old prints, and above the seven-foot servery (behind which are the beer casks) are a bow and arrows. With such an excellent choice of well-kept ales, it is no surprise that the pub is a regular in major good beer guides. Landlord (for five years) Tim Park spent the previous five years as a barman, and clearly knows his subject. He welcomes children to the large garden, which has swings and climbing frame. Indoor amusements are in the form of bar skittles, darts, shove ha'penny and a quiz on Monday evenings.

THE FLOWER POTS INN

Cheriton, nr Alresford.   Tel. (0962) 771318

        Location: Near village centre on Beauworth road.
   Credit cards: Not accepted.
 Accommodation: 2 doubles, 3 twins en suite. TV, tea & coffee. £18pp. Campers welcome.
         Bitters: Archers Village, Ballards Best, Hop Back Summer Lighting, guest.
          Lagers: Fosters.

Examples of bar meals (lunch & evening, except Sun. evening): *beef stew, chilli, jacket potatoes, ploughman's, sandwiches, daily specials eg sweet & sour chicken with egg fried rice.*

An unpretentious, simple country inn, this, yet quite out-of-the-ordinary. Beer from small local breweries is drawn straight from the barrels behind the bar, and plans are in hand to build a mini brewery on site, so it comes as no surprise that plaudits have been won from leading good beer and pub guides. Customers are also very satisfied, witnessed by an ever growing bar meal trade, and the accommodation is well filled most weekends. This is housed in a converted stable block; the rooms are light and modern, well-equipped but modestly priced. The inn was built in 1848 as a farmhouse, and attractive period features include a terra cotta floor, open brick fireplace, milk churn in the lounge and a very deep glass-covered well in the bar. Also exceptional is the fact that it has been with the same family for 25 years, the last two or so with Paul, Jo, Pat and Bob the happy spaniel. Children are welcome in the large, pleasant garden with views over fields and woods. Darts, crib and shove ha'penny. Ramblers note: the Southdown Way, Wayfarer's Walk and Itchen Way all converge on Cheriton.

Hampshire

THE HAWKLEY INN

Pococks Lane, Hawkley, West Liss.   Tel. (0730 84) 205
         Location: Near village green.
      Credit cards: Access, Visa, Mastercard.
           Bitters: Ballards Best & Trotton, Hogsback TEA, Ringwood 49,
                     guests.
            Lagers: Stella Artois, Carlsberg.

Examples of bar meals (lunch & evening, except Sun evening): *homemade soup, lasagne, coronation chicken, quiches, omelettes, salads, ploughman's, jacket potatoes, rolls, daily specials eg turkey pie, beef casserole. Apple pie, cheesecake.*
Examples of restaurant meals (as above): *fricasse of mushrooms & garlic in filo pastry, grilled sea bass with garlic & herb butter, chicken breast in apricot almond & cream sauce, fillet of beef en croute with madeira sauce, vegetarian strudel with spinach cream sauce.*

A moose gazes out from the pub sign and its enormous stuffed counterpart hangs over the fireplace (with roaring log fire in winter) in the bar. It is a silent witness to much activity, for this is a very lively and popular freehouse run by Ev Collins for the last two or three years. Good food - well above typical pub fare - is one important draw, but there's also a very good selection of local and guest ales. Children are welcome and an area is set aside for non-smokers, but in summer one can make use of the large, safe garden with Wendy house and barbecues for Sunday lunch. The countryside is lovely, and many walkers drop by for refreshment, perhaps following 'Hangers Walk.' Music is performed lived two or three times per month. Bar billiards.

THE THREE HORSESHOES

Elsted, nr Midhurst.   Tel. (0730) 825746
      Location: Village centre, 4 miles south west of Midhurst.
  Credit cards: Access, Visa, Mastercard.
       Bitters: Fullers London Pride, Highgate Dark, Ballards, Wadworth 6X, Youngs Special, Bass.
       Lagers: Carling, Tennents Extra.

Examples of bar meals (lunch & evening except Sun. evening): *homemade soups, pigeon casserole, roast pheasant, steak & Guinness pie, cottage pie, fresh sole, plaice, vegetable lasagne, jacket potatoes, salads, ploughman's, sandwiches. Homemade puddings. Special fish evenings planned. Trad. Sun. roasts.*

Re-opening only in December 1992 (after refurbishment), this characterful 16th-century inn should do well under new licensees Andrew and Sue Beavis. Their loyal followers at their other pub, The Bull's Head at Fishbourne, will vouch for that. As well as dispensing an excellent range of beers, food is fresh and homecooked, chalked daily on a blackboard. In a peaceful spot three miles off the main road, the building remains almost untouched by the 20th century. Enter the low front door (taking care not to let the chickens in!), you will find yourself in a cosy, timbered, split-level interior, made up of small, low-ceiling rooms, one of which has an inglenook and another serves as a dining room. You will not find a jukebox; entertainment is in the form of pub games. The south-facing garden commands lovely views over the Downs. Children (welcome inside) will love the rabbits, but beware of the white one - it bites!

THE ROYAL OAK

Hooksway, Chilgrove.   Tel. (0243 59) 257
          Location: 1½ miles north of Chilgrove, off B2414.
      Credit cards: Access, Visa, Diners, Amex.
  Accommodation: Camping only.
           Bitters: Ruddles County & Best, Gibbs Mews Bishop's Tipple, Courage Directors, Websters Yorkshire, guests. Guinness. Lagers: Holsten, Carlsberg. Plus Scrumpy Jack cider.

Examples of bar meals (lunch & evening, 7 days): *homemade venison pie, steak & kidney pie, steaks & grills, chilli, lasagne, king prawns, broccoli & cream cheese pie, mushroom nut & bean caserole, ploughman's. Bramble pie, rhum baba.*
Examples from Hideaway Restaurant menu (evenings Tues - Sat plus Sun lunch): *terrine of wood pigeon, ratatouille omelette with gruyere cheese, monkfish & vegetable parcels, steaks, roast guinea fowl, rack of lamb, roast saddle of rabbit on bed of spinach with port & mushroom sauce, medallions of venison served on crouton (topped with pate & coated with red wine sauce).*

You probably won't find Hooksway on your road map; at the foot of a narrow lane, surrounded by woods, it comprises just one house and this 15th century pub and restaurant. But it is has been host to three monarchs, no less, together on the same shooting party, and to many thousands of humbler folk who come for the wonderful tranquility, good food and ales. Game naturally features prominently on the menu. The lower bar (or tap room) seats 20, has polished brick floor and is ideal for walkers. The main bar is beamed and has an open fire. Live jazz is played on the last Friday of each month and there is live entertainment (eg folk singing, Morris dancing) most other Fridays. Children are welcome, and the large garden has play equipment and barbecue.

THE RICHMOND ARMS

Mill Lane, West Ashling, nr Chichester.　　　　　　　　Tel. (0243) 575730
　　　Location:　In village.
　Credit cards:　Not accepted.
　　　　Bitters:　Everchanging guests; Marston's Pedigree, Timothy Taylor Landlord, Harveys Sussex Mild, Boddingtons, Brakspears, King & Barnes Festive, Thwaites Traditional.
　　　　Lagers:　Edehall Export, Stella Artois, Heineken, Heineken Export.

Examples of bar meals (lunch & evening, 7 days): *chicken tikka, fish pie, local trout, mixed grill, steaks, stuffed plaice with prawns, chicken Kiev, Richmond burger, veg lasagne, vegetable pie, moussaka, rack of lamb, jacket potatoes, salads, ploughman's, sandwiches. Treacle pudding, hot chocolate fudge cake, fruit salad. Children's menu.*
NB. *Open all day Sunday in summer*

An amazing 127 different real ales have passed through the pumps here in under one year since Bob and Chris took over, and 545 in the eight years before that. So it's a Mecca for beer drinkers, but there's much else besides. Built around 1850, this is not the most eyecatching of pubs, but nonetheless does not lack character, and is much in favour with actors from the Chichester theatre. Ducks form the main theme of decor, and the collection of decoys in the bar is used for an annual charity race down a local stream. Food is traditional and wholesome, with an already large menu about to be augmented with a vegetarian selection. Theme nights like St.Patrick's or Burns' add further novelty. Children are welcome, and by the car park is a patio with pergola. Praised by national good pub guide.

THE LAMB INN

West Wittering, nr Chichester.   Tel. (0243) 511105
        Location: On B2179 towards Birdham.
    Credit cards: Access, Visa.
          Bitters: Ballards Ringwood, Bunce, guests.
          Lagers: Becks, Carlsberg, Newquay Steam.

Examples from lunchtime menu (every day, snacks only on Sunday): *steak & mushroom pie, smoked fish flan, lasagne, fried plaice, chicken cordon bleu, spinach & mushroom bake, ploughman's, toasted sandwiches, salad bar in season.*
Examples from evening menu (not Suns): *some dishes as above, sirloin steak, grilled halibut/lemon sole/plaice, gammon, vegetable bake. Apricot & almond tart, chocolate glu glu sponge, treacle tart.*

It is hard to find fault with this 18th-century inn, well run by Nigel and Jo Carter. Originally a cottage and forge, it was recognised as a pub in 1835, and known as The Lambert & Norris. A favourite amongst boaters from Chichester harbour and holidaymakers from the sandy beaches, the Lamb is also well regarded by the 'natives' and by national good pub guides. Home cooking and good beer have much to do with this, coupled with a warm atmosphere - especially when the log and coal fires are lit. Attractive local photos decorate the bar, which has polished parquet flooring, and the three-in-one dining room (children permitted), luxuriously carpeted in two parts, the third being the garden room with summer salad bar. Barbecues. Car park.

THE BLACK HORSE

Birdham Road, Apuldram, nr Chichester.   Tel. (0243) 784068

     Location: On A286.
 Credit cards: Acces, Visa.
      Bitters: King & Barnes, Burtons, John Bull.
       Lagers: Lowenbrau, Castlemaine, Skol.

Examples of bar meals (lunch & evening, 7 days): *deep fried calamari, king prawns, baked camembert, deep fried seafood, lasagne, roasts, steaks & grills, jacket potatoes, salads, ploughman's, sandwiches, daily specials. Trad. Sun. roasts.*

"Always a warm welcome, and a great meal at a price that's right" - the declared aim of the management. The cheerful young staff do generate a friendly atmosphere, and the very sizeable menu is moderately priced. Although drawing trade on the way to the beaches of Wittering, it is also well frequented by locals. Built as cottages around 1775, it became a pub circa 1890, but its origins are clearly evident from the old beams, inglenooks and brickwork, decorated with agricultural implements. A separate dining area seats about 25, and the large garden with patio has benches and tables. Families are most welcome, and there's parking for about 60 cars. Chichester and its harbour are only about three miles away. Rated by CAMRA guide.

West Sussex

THE GEORGE & DRAGON

Burpham, nr Arundel.   Tel. (0903) 883131
        Location: At end of village (no through road).
   Credit cards: Access, Visa.
         Bitters: Harveys, Courage Directors, Ruddles County, 2 guests.
          Lagers: Fosters, Kronenbourg, Carlsberg.

Examples of bar meals (lunch & evening, except Sun evening): *steaks, chicken breast stuffed with garlic, catch of the day, vegetarian dish, ploughman's, sandwiches, b/board specials eg meat & vegetable crumble, spicy pork fillet & rice.*
Examples of restaurant meals (evenings except Sun): *smoked trout mousse with Pernod, pigeon & walnut salad; Scotch fillet stuffed with smoked oysters (in puff pastry on piquant sauce), fillets of sole stuffed with duxelle & prawns (served with dill & vermouth sauce), butterleberli (Swiss speciality). Homemade desserts.*

A most enjoyable drive to this exquisite little village (in lovely walking country) is rewarded by marvellous views over Arundel Castle to the sea beyond. The road leads nowhere else, but visitors are drawn by this gastronomic jewel, employing two first-class chefs (one Cordon Bleu), lauded by Egon Ronay, CAMRA and other good pub guides, and recipient of an AA two-star knife and fork rating. Owned by the West family for 350 years until 1945 (one of whom is said to linger on in spirit), this old alehouse was a smugglers haunt; George West (a blacksmith) kept order by thumping the table. Look for the old twister - not the landlord, but a gaming device on the ceiling used to divide their spoils. W.G. Grace would have supped here after playing on the adjacent pitch. Truly, this is a house of exceptional quality and character. Amiable proprietors George and Marianne Walker allow well behaved children.

THE CROWN INN

Pulborough Road, Cootham, nr Storrington. Tel. (0903) 742625

  Location: 1 mile west of Storrington on A283.
 Credit cards: Visa, Mastercard, Amex.
   Bitters: Flowers Original, Strongs Country, Marstons Pedigree, Wadworth 6X.
   Lagers: Heineken, Stella Artois.

Examples of bar meals (lunch & evening, 7 days): *curry, lasagne, chilli, scampi, cod, plaice, omelettes, seafood & vegetarian crepes, jacket potatoes, ploughman's, sandwiches, daily specials.*

Examples of restaurant meals (as above): *spare ribs marinaded in Pernod, brochette of lamb marinaded in coriander & garlic with almond rice, breast of chicken tikka, prime steaks, daily specials eg medallions of fillet steak in Drambuie sauce. Celebrated for local game, fresh fish on Fridays. Trad. Sun. roasts.*

The Southdown Way runs very close by, and many a weary traveller has sought rest and refreshment here at the foot of the Downs over the past 700 years. Parts of the original building still stand, the beams and open fire inducing a feeling of comfort and well-being. This will be further enhanced by an excellent choice of ales and quality homecooked food, local game being a winter speciality. Note that children are welcome in the restaurant and that reservations are taken. The garden has a play area, and indoor pastimes include bar billiards, darts, pool and shove ha'penny. Barbecues and other special events are arranged on occasion, but there's always plenty of other attractions: Parham Park, with its fine house and gardens, is just 200 yards, and Arundel Castle, Bignor Roman Villa, Southdown Gliding Club and West Sussex Golf Club are all within easy reach.

West Sussex

THE WHITE HART

Stopham Bridge, Pulborough.   Tel. (0798) 873321
    Location: On A283 (old road) 1 mile west of Pulborough.
  Credit cards: Access, Visa.
     Bitters: Flowers, guest.
      Lagers: Stella Artois, Heineken.

Examples of bar meals (lunch & evening, 7 days, except Sunday evenings in winter): *homemade fish pie, meat/veg lasagne, cod, spicy sausages, hungryman's platter, angler's platter; fresh spinach ravioli, baked potatoes, sandwiches, daily specials eg steak & ale pie* .
Examples of restaurant meals (as above): *gateau of fresh brill & sliced scallops, sole & salmon roulade with lobster sauce; red snapper Cantonese, Atlantic shark steak au poivre, sirloin steak, blackboard specials eg chef's game casserole with herb dumplings, platter of locally smoked & cured fish.*

Seafood Pub Restaurant of the Year 1991/92 (London and South East Region), The White Hart's menu presents a problem: what to have from such an enormous choice, which includes the familiar along with the exotic, such as Seychelles Bourgeous, Vara-Vara, Mahi-Mahi and many more. Also rare is the pub itself; listed in Domesday, it was an alehouse in the 16th century and what was the forge is now the dining room. Landlady (for 10 years) Linda Collier welcomes children, and there's play equipment in the large garden. This is bordered by the River Arun (the pub has fishing rights), spanned by a fine medieval stone bridge. Barbecues are held Sunday evenings in summer, but there's a full year-round programme of special events (eg Creole, Tyrolean, Carol Singing) often with live entertainment. Recommended by Egon Ronay and others.

THE ANGEL HOTEL

Angel Street, Petworth.   Tel. (0798) 42153

        Location: 200 yards east of town centre on Pulborough road.
    Credit cards: Visa, Amex, Switch.
 Accommodation: 6 doubles, 3 family. 1 wheelchair-friendly. All with private facilities, tv's, trouser press, hair dryer, tea & coff. T.B. 3-crowns. From £30 single, £40 double incl.
         Bitters: Ballards, Tanglefoot, Batemans, Adnams, Badger.
          Lagers: Stella Artois, Carlsberg Export, Fosters, Munchener, Schmucker.

Examples of bar meals (lunch & evening, 7 days): *moules mariniere, steaks, fresh grilled lemon sole/plaice, omelettes, quiche, vegetarian bake, ploughman's.*
Examples of restaurant/carvery meals (as above): *haunch of venison, forerib of beef, Norfolk turkey, curry, deep fried plaice stuffed with prawns in cream sauce. Profiteroles, bread & butter pudding, treacle tart.* Trad. Sun roasts £8.95 (1 course). Bistro fixed-price supper menu (evenings only): *caillettes of spinach & pork terrine, fresh fish, rack of lamb with Dijon mustard, escalope of veal flambeed with Armagnac.*

One almost expects to see Mr Pickwick warming himself by the roaring fire; genial landlord Mervyn Church would be pleased to greet him. His is a coaching inn of rare character, 13th-century and charged with an atmosphere often lacking in a group hotel. The Pilgrim Fathers rested here on their way to Portsmouth; they would recognise it still today, although standards of comfort and food far surpass their expectations. Magnificent Petworth House is just a five-minute walk, but the bolder may like to try the all-in package, including a flight in a hot-air balloon! Champagne days out at Goodwood. Children welcome - walled garden. Functions well catered for.

West Sussex

THE HALF MOON INN

Kirdford, nr Billingshurst.   Tel. (0403 77) 223

Location:	Opposite 12th-century church.
Credit cards:	Access, Visa, Mastercard, Eurocard, Switch.
Accommodation:	1 double/twin, 1 family. Tea & coffee. £30 per room.
Bitters:	Old Speckled Hen, Wadworth 6X, Flowers OB, Boddingtons, Whitbread.
Lagers:	Heineken, Stella Artois.

Examples of bar/restaurant meals (lunch & evening, except Sun evenings; restaurant closed Mon evenings): *oysters, mussels, fish soup, smoked venison, Mexican chilli bean soup, Dover sole, tuna steak in sauce, chicken curry, sirloin steak, lentil chilli, scabboard fish with chilli & garlic. Trad. Sun. roasts.*

Although near Billingshurst, it's Billingsgate which is important to the Moran family - connections with the fish market go back 130 years. Hence it is no surprise to find fresh seafood prominent on the menu, homecooked, of course. Kirdford is an exceptionally pretty village and is also fortunate to have this agreeable inn, actually more appealing inside than out. A superb inglenook is one outstanding feature, and look for three old hats hanging on an antler. The family run the business with verve and enthusiasm; they will help arrange just about anything:- clay pigeon shoots, golfing, Goodwood, tennis (at the inn), ballooning, go-karts, private parties, outside catering (a speciality) and of course weddings - very handy with the church just opposite! If this were not enough, there are frequent special events and theme evenings, plus barbecues when the sun shines. Children welcome and have play equipment in garden. Games room.

THE FOX INN

Bucks Green, Rudgwick.   Tel. (0403) 822386

     Location: On A281 Horsham to Guildford road.
Credit cards: Not accepted.
       Bitters: King & Barnes Best, Sussex, Broadwood, Festive, Old Ale.
       Lagers: Carling, Holsten Export. Plus Stowford Press cider.

Examples of bar meals (lunch & evening, except Sun evening): *homemade soups, beef teryaki (noted), grilled trout stuffed with prawns, homemade chicken Kiev, steaks, pizzas, burgers, lasagne, scampi, plaice, leeks in mustard sauce, vegetable pie, jacket potatoes, salads, ploughman's, sandwiches. Banana split, death by chocolate, sorbets. Children's menu. Trad. Sun. roasts in winter.*

Once a year a pony is led through the inn, to acknowledge a bridleway between front and back doors. Other time-honoured traditions are also well observed at this friendly village local, formerly 16th-century cottages. Pauline (ex air-hostess) and Charlie (ex restaurateur) serve a wide range of fresh, homecooked food, English and international, plus excellent beers. In 1930 the son of the then landlord died, and is said to return every Boxing Day. He will find it warm and comfortable, the saloon bar dominated by a large inglenook, and the main bar with its collections of books, bottles and pictures. A small games room has pool, darts and skittles, quiz nights are held on the first Sunday of the month, and local groups perform on Wednesday evenings. Children are welcome in the large garden, which has climbing frame and swings, and barbecues Sunday lunchtimes in summer.

West Sussex

THE SELSEY ARMS

Coolham, nr Horsham.   Tel. (0403) 741537
      Location: At crossroads on A272, 4 miles east of Billinghurst.
  Credit cards: Not accepted.
        Bitters: Wadworth 6X, King & Barnes Sussex, Strongs Country, Morlands Old Speckled Hen
        Lagers: Heineken, Heineken Export.

Examples of bar meals (lunch & evening, 7 days): *homemade bacon & lentil soup, steak & kidney pie, chicken & broccoli pie, cauliflower cheese, rump steak, gammon, plaice, ploughman's, sandwiches, fresh fish, delicious fish pies. Chocolate fudge cake, icecreams.*

The King of Prussia is said to have once been a landlord of this honest 16th century village pub; it was part of the huge Selsey estate that stretched all the way to Goodwood. His successor for the past nine years has been ebullient Tony Woods, who in earlier times could have been the blacksmith working in the forge which is now an outbuilding. Tony's immediate predecessor, Roy (landlord for 30 years), is still a regular and a fount of local history. Such continuity is sadly all too rare these days, but the pub has the character to entice one to stay: flagstone floors, exposed beams and brickwork, roaring log fires in the inglenooks. There's also a good collection of brass and a spinning jenny mounted on a ceiling. Children are welcome and the 1/2-acre garden (with barbecue) is sheltered and safe. Darts. No jukebox or piped misic.

West Sussex

THE BLUE SHIP

The Haven, Billingshurst.   Tel. (0403) 822709
       Location: Off road between Five Oaks (A29) and Bucks Green (A281) at haven, signposted Gibbons Mill and Garlands.
  Credit cards: Not accepted.
        Bitters: King & Barnes, Sussex, K & B Broadwood. Plus Guinness.
        Lagers: Carling, Holsten Export. Plus Stowford Press cider.

Examples of bar meals (lunch & evening, except Sun & Mon evenings): *homemade soups, cheesey cottage pie, ratatouille au gratin, lasagne, cod, plaice, scampi, steak & kidney pie, chilli, ploughman's, sandwiches. Fruit crumble, Granny's wedding cake, treacle tart, chocolate fudge cake.*

Others lay claim to being 'real country pubs', but here is the genuine article, built around 1500. Enter by a low door and a cheerful face will greet you at the servery hatch opposite. Beer is served direct from the casks, not pumped. At times the bar is full of working dogs and their owners, the once white ceilings are now yellow, and all is much as you might have found it around 1900. The solid old beams are bedecked with foreign banknotes, the floors are polished brick, and furniture is scrubbed wood. A games room has bar billiards and darts, and a small dining room is decorated with pictures of large dogs - landlady Jenny Davie has six Newfoundlands and is a judge. She has also supervised the cooking since arriving five years ago with husband John. They welcome children and have a garden with play equipment. Featured in national good pub guide.

West Sussex

THE FOUNTAIN INN

Ashurst, Steyning. Tel. (0403) 710219
Location: On B2135 between Partridge Green and Steyning.
Credit cards: Not accepted.
Bitters: Fremlins, Strong Country, Marston's Pedigree, Flowers Original, 2 guests.
Lagers: Stella Artois, Heineken.

Examples from lunchtime menu (7 days): *homemade steak & kidney pie, cottage pie, lasagne verdi, moussaka, quiche, flans, sauasages, ploughman's, daily specials.* Examples from 'candlelit supper' menu (not Wed. or Sun.): *steaks, chicken Kiev, turkey cordon bleu, curry, scampi, cod. Oriental barbecues in summer and Oriental theme evenings in winter.*

Voted "Best Country Pub in West Sussex" (1990) in a competition organised by The Brewers Society and Brighton Evening Argus; voted no. 2 CAMRA pub in the south of England (1990); a regular in good beer and pub guides; used by Paul McCartney as a film location and by Laurence Olivier as his 'local'; clearly, here is no run-of-the-mill freehouse. For 15 years Maurice and Jean Caine, both from an aviation background, have run this unspoilt 16th century inn, full of character and atmosphere. Even the ghost is friendly, and has reportedly been seen in daylight more than once. Low beams, flagstone floors and inglenooks are unmistakably authentic. A jukebox would be sacrilege, but there are quieter pursuits like shove ha'penny and crib. Children are allowed in the lounge if eating, and there is a large garden with duck pond and play equipment. The new Oriental-style cooking is proving extremely popular.

West Sussex

ANSTY CROSS INN

Cuckfield Road, Ansty, nr Haywards Heath.   Tel. (0444) 413038
      Location: Village centre, jncn of A272 with B2036.
   Credit cards: Access, Visa.
       Bitters: Ruddles County & Best, Websters.
       Lagers: Fosters, Carlsberg, Holsten Export.

Examples of bar meals (lunch & evening, 7 days): *chilli, pizza, steaks, mixed grill, chicken Kiev, Scottish salmon, lasagne, macaroni cheese with various toppings, sweet & sour pork, steak & kidney pie, self-serve salads, ploughman's, many daily specials eg tandoori chicken, tuna & cheese pie, homemade quiche. Banoffi pie, hot chocolate fudge cake, apple pie. Children's menu. Trad. Sun. roasts in winter.*

There has certainly been an inn at these busy crossroads since time immemorial, and this one was built around the turn of the century on the site of the 'Green Cross Inn' (the pub sign depicts a scene from the Bayeux tapestry showing the Conqueror with a papal banner bearing a green cross. The emblem was adopted by a local nobleman named Hussey). Its light, uncluttered interior, nicely furnished in pine, consists of a comfortable lounge bar, games room and pleasant 35-seater dining room (children welcome). Landlord Steve Tickner is an accomplished cook and, given notice, will prepare anything to customer requirements. With Wendy, he came here in January 1990, and has maintained a place in influential good pub guides. Colourful, safe garden has play area. Car park.

THE CROWN

The Green, Horsted Keynes, nr Haywards Heath. Tel. (0825) 790449
  Location: Village centre, five miles north of Haywards Heath.
  Credit cards: Visa, Mastercard.
  Bitters: Harveys, Tetley, Burton.
  Lagers: Castlemaine, Carlsberg, Carlsberg Hof, Lowenbrau.

Examples of bar meals (lunch & evening, 7 days): *homemade steak & kidney pie, Chinese stir-fried prawns, homecooked ham & egg, French style mushroom crepes, mushroom & nut fetuccini, daily specials.*
Examples of restaurant meals (Fri & Sat evenings, Sun lunch): *mushroom provencale, whitebait with yoghurt & watercress dip, tiger prawns served with rice & stir-fry vegetables, sirloin steak with garlic prawns, breast of chicken in port wine & mushroom sauce, Crown grill. Trad Sun. roasts.*

There are some little-heard-of activities here for those who like a spot of recreation with their refreshments: a stoolball pitch, for example, along with cricket, and inside is pool and darts. The games are in the public bar, but the lounge bar is more conversational, with exposed timbers, inglenook fireplace and horsebrasses. Tim and Rose Rapley have refurbished this 15th-century pub to create two bars and a restaurant in delightful surroundings. There is a furnished garden and facilities for the children and dogs. Bluebell Steam Railway and beautiful Sheffield Park nearby.

THE FOX & HOUNDS

Fox Hill, Haywards Heath.   Tel. (0444) 413342

      Location: On Ditchling road, approx 1 mile from town.
 Credit cards: Access, Visa, Diners, Amex.
       Bitters: Ruddles County & Best, Flowers Original, Websters Yorkshire.
       Lagers: Holsten, Carlsberg, Fosters.

Examples of bar/restaurant meals (lunch & evening, 7 days): *butterfly prawns, turkey ham & leek pie, steak & kidney pie, haddock & prawn smokies, curry, steaks, trout grilled with bacon, tomato & veg tagliatelle. Chocolate trufitos, charlotte russe, apple pie. Carvery Thurs - Sat evening & Sun lunch.*

Although not an unattractive building from the outside, the interior of this 16th-century coaching inn is most agreeable. Its long three-tiered lounge bar is overlooked by a gallery (with seating), and smartly polished wood is much in evidence. The arrangement of tables and chairs lends itself to conversation, but one section has bar billiards and there is also a children's room. The restaurant is a splendid room, with high vaulted ceiling and whirring fans, thickly carpeted floors and flowers on each table. A reputation for good food is well established, and the carvery is a popular feature. So, too, are barbecues, held in the pleasant, sheltered garden, which has a play area. Large car park. Not far from lovely Sheffield Park and Bluebell Railway.

THE PELHAM ARMS

High Street, Lewes. Tel. (0273) 476149
- Location: Top of High Street.
- Credit cards: Access, Visa.
- Bitters: King & Barnes Sussex, Festive, Broadwood, Old Ale.
- Lagers: Castlemaine, Carling, Holsten Export.

Examples of bar/Restaurant meals (lunch & evening, Mon - Sat): *at time of writing menus are undergoing total revision. The intention is to offer an even wider range of quality home cooked food.*

Voted "Sussex Pub of the Year" by the Evening Argus a couple of years ago, the Pelham is well known throughout the county for the range of good local ales, outstanding home cooking and well above average wine list. Another important draw is the rather agreeable 'old world' atmosphere, established by the 17th century oak in the lounge and pine effect 'Sussex kitchen' in the restaurant area, warmed from a large open fireplace. It all once belonged to the Pelham family, and still has close associations with the horse racing fraternity, but Martin and Alison Shaw are pleased to welcome allcomers of all ages, from high chair to wheel chair. Sunday evening sees live entertainment, and barbecues are held in the car park in summer.

East Sussex

THE HALFWAY HOUSE

Rose Hill, Isfield, nr Uckfield. Tel. (082 575) 382
      Location: On A26 between Uckfield and Lewes.
  Credit cards: Not accepted.
       Bitters: Harveys Best, IPA & Old.
        Lagers: Carling, Tuborg.

Examples of bar meals (lunch & evening, 7 days): *large variety of steaks with or without sauces, lobster, lemon sole, Dover sole, trout, fresh salmon in sauce, halibut, cod, scampi, seafood platter, mussels, langoustines, turkey & ham pie, steak & kidney pie, curry, lasagne, omelettes, vegetarian quiche, vegetable pie, salads, ploughman's.*

'Halfway' between Tunbridge Wells and Brighton, this 17th-century coaching inn has long been a favourite stop for the weary traveller seeking rest and refreshment. In winter warm yourself by the real fires, as generations before have done, and absorb the cottagey atmosphere under the same sturdy timbers. Darts, pool, dominoes, and scrabble are amongst the diversions, or in summer you may see a classic car auction. The large, attractive garden has plenty of seating, and ball games may be played in an adjoining field. The range and quality of the food far surpasses that known to travellers past, seafood being a speciality, and the ale is rated by a national good beer guide. Although there is no formal restaurant, tables are laid up and may be reserved. Licensees of six years, Mike and Caroline Simpson, welcome children and organise barbecues and other seasonal activities.

East Sussex

THE SHEFFIELD COACH HOUSE

Sheffield Green, Danehill   Tel: (0825) 790160
        Location: On A275 from East Grinstead to Lewes.
   Credit Cards: Access, Visa, Mastercard
         Bitters: Harveys, Stones, Worthington
          Lagers: Tennents, Tennents Extra

Examples of bar meals (lunch & evening, 7 days): *homemade soups, steak & kidney pie, lamb & mushroom stew, roast, steaks, garlic chicken, curry, fresh fish, scampi, ravioli, savoury rolls, jacket potatoes, ploughman's.*
Examples of restaurant meals (lunch and evening except Sun evening): *duck breast chow-chow, steak teryaki, king prawns Creole, lemon sole, local trout. Jam roly-poly, bread & butter pudding, apple & raisin pie. Trad. Sun roasts.*

Sheffield Park gardens are especially lovely in autumn; you will likely have seen them depicted in books and calendars. Part of the estate, this 18th-century coaching inn (under new management) stands less than one mile from them and the famous Bluebell Steam Railway. But it has attractions of its own: a skittle alley can take parties of up to 40 and the restaurant is ideal for weddings and other functions; the three bars, timbered and with open fires and brickwork, each have a theme – the Cricketers, the Dickens and the Stable (with pool and darts). Children are welcome and have a plethora of play equipment in the garden. Dinner dances are a regular event, and singles nights are planned for Fridays.

East Sussex

THE PLOUGH & HORSES

Walshes Road, Crowborough.   Tel. (0892) 652614

Location:	Between Crowborough and Jarvis Brook.
Credit cards:	Access, Visa.
Bitters:	Wadworth 6X, Youngs Special & IPA, Harveys, King & Barnes, Tetley.
Lagers:	Lowenbrau, Skol, Castlemaine, Tennents & Tennents Extra, Carling.

Examples of bar meals (lunch & evening, 7 days): *homemade soups, steak sandwich, omelettes, salads, ploughman's, daily specials.*
Examples of restaurant meals (as above): *steaks with various sauces, venison in rich red wine sauce, grilled halibut, Dover sole, Greenland wild salmon, trout meuniere, roast poussin (in white wine, lemon & tarragon sauce), half roast duck in orange & morello cherry sauce, daily specials.* Trad. Sun. roasts £8.95.

This is Winnie the Pooh country, as immortalised by A.A. Milne, and the bridge over the little stream where he played 'Pooh sticks' is not far from here. It's a delightful corner of our countryside, on the edge of Ashdown Forest, and one of the highest points in Sussex. Tucked away down a country lane, yet only five minutes from Crowborough, this friendly old inn (circa 1700) has been a labour of love for David and Brenda Newton, who have made it one of the most successful in the area. Simple bar food is supplemented by a sizeable and diverse menu in the 48-seater restaurant, with a good inexpensive wine list to match. Children have their own room, but in summer may prefer the garden with play area and barbecue. Car parking.

THE DORSET ARMS

Withyham.   Tel. (0892) 770278
- Location: On B2110.
- Credit cards: Access, Visa.
- Bitters: Harveys Best, IPA.
- Lagers: Tuborg, Carling.

Examples of bar meals (French bread only Sun - Tues evenings): *lamb cutlets, chicken Kiev, scampi, plaice, jumbo sausages, veg lasagne, salads, ploughman's (noted), daily specials eg chicken in mustard sauce.*
Examples of restaurant meals (not Tues - Sun evenings): *deep fried brie with raspberry sauce, steaks, chicken stuffed with leek & stilton, grilled Dover sole, scampi provencale, trout. Homemade apple pie, crumbles. Trad. Sun. roasts.*

Lords and ladies rub shoulders with farm workers, and nobody puts on airs and graces at this unpretentious country pub. Built in 1556, it is named after the famous Sackville family, earls of Dorset, but there are more interesting tales to tell. Percy, a cavalier when he was alive, is said to generate his own 'ambience', and was even seen to stoke up the fire one night! An axe once fell off the wall unaided, and on the day of the funeral of one of the regulars a robin flew in the bar and alighted on his chair, fulfilling an old superstition in these parts. If all this sounds a little spooky, it is in fact a notably relaxed place, with friendly bar staff and a chef who is prepared to be flexible to meet customer requirements. Children are welcome in the Delaware Restaurant (can be reserved for functions), where a now broken axe hangs over a fireplace unusual for having a window in it.

East Sussex

THE GOLDEN GALLEON

Exceat Bridge, Seaford.   Tel. (0323) 892247

      Location: On A259 towards Eastbourne.
 Credit cards: Not accepted.
        Bitters: Courage Best & Directors, Yorkshire, guest.
        Lagers: Kronenbourg, Hofmeister, Fosters.

Examples of bar meals (lunch & evening, 7 days): Italian seafood salad, bruschetta (garlic bread topped with plum tomatoes), chicken in tomato & fresh ginger sauce, fresh local fish, steaks, self-serve salad, ploughman's, daily specials eg pasta bake, lasagne, stilton & broccoli quiche.

There's more than a touch of the Italian 'trattoria' here on this lovely stretch of coast, once earmarked as a likely invasion point from Europe. Proprietors Stefano and Lindsey Diella set out seven years ago to blend the best of British with continental style, and would seem to have done so successfully, judging by their local popularity and the plaudits from national guides. Recently they were recipients of the 'Heartbeat' award for healthy eating and hygiene. Some Italian dishes, like lasagne, have been almost hijacked by the English, but Stefano says come and try the real thing! You will find yourself in an attractive bar cum dining room, half set aside for non-smokers, with high vaulted ceilings and timbers rescued from shipwrecks. On summer evenings you may prefer to take in the glorious views from the terrace, and perhaps develop an appetite with a leisurely stroll to the beach. Well behaved children welcome.

East Sussex

THE STAR INN

Norman's Bay, Pevensey.　　　　　　　　　　　Tel. (0323) 762648
　　　　Location:　On the bay.
　Credit cards:　Access, Visa.
　　　　　Bitters:　Harveys, Chas Wells Bombadier, Bass, Worthington, Youngs, Old Roger, Gales HSB, Tanglefoot, guests.
　　　　　Lagers:　Red Stripe, Hofmeister, Warsteiner, Carling, Tennents Extra, Carlsberg Export.

Examples of bar/restaurant meals (lunch & evening, 7 days): *roast pheasant, poached salmon, steak & kidney pie, lamb Shrewsbury, chicken & asparagus pie, sausages in Yorkshire pudding, steaks, selection of fresh local fish, 6 vegetarian dishes, salads, ploughman's, baguettes, daily specials. 20 homemade desserts.*

The bloodiest of all battles between smugglers and customs men took place here one dark night in 1828. Although the blockade was broken, many lay dead, and an era which had lasted over 200 years was effectively at an end. The inn was almost 500 years old even then, but though renowned for its matchless smuggling connections, is today one of the most successful in the county on the strength of good home-cooking and ales. The two bars and 90-seater restaurant are well used, and the venerable beams shake a little to the syncopated rythmns of live jazz every Tuesday and Sunday lunchtime, but without detriment to the unique and ancient character. Custodians of all this history for the last ten years have been Francis and Mary Maynard, who welcome children and have a garden with play area and barbecue.

THE WAR-BILL-IN-TUN INN

Warbleton, nr Heathfield. Tel. (0435) 830636
    Location: Opposite church.
    Credit cards: Access, Visa.
    Bitters: Harveys Best, John Smiths, Old Ale in winter, guests.
    Lagers: Holsten, Fosters, Stella Artois.

Examples of bar/restaurant meals (lunch & evening 7 days, but no bar food Sat evenings): *smoked oysters, salmon steak with seafood sauce, grilled trout with almond & wine sauce, steaks, Gressingham duck in orange sauce, veal escalope with mushroom & cream sauce, homemade steak & kidney pie, curry, scampi, salads, meat platters, blackboard specials. Apricot & brandy gateau, chocolate & rum gateau, banoffie pie. Trad. Sun. roasts.*

The odd name would seem to be a play on 'Warbleton' (said to be England's smallest village), but there is a story that it derives from civil war soldiers smashing open a barrel (or tun) with an axe. If that sounds unlikely there are many more tales about priest holes, sudden death and ghosts (a 17th-century lady) which, sitting round the log fire in the depths of winter, do not seem too far fetched. Indeed, it would be unusual if an alehouse built in the late 13th century did not boast a few blood curdling stories, but none will detract from the enjoyment of the first rate cooking and convivial atmosphere which has won a place in local affections and national guides. Credit for this goes to Bryan and Valerie Whitton, who've served behind their serpent-shaped bar for over seven years. Children welcome by arrangement, garden to front and rear.

THE CHERRY TREE

Dale Hill, Ticehurst.   Tel. (0580) 201229

         Location: From Flimwell traffic lights on A21 take Ticehurst to Wadhurst road and circle the one way system.
  Credit cards: Access, Visa.
Accommodation: All rooms en suite, with tv, tea & coffee.
          Bitters: Harveys, Adnams, Ruddles.
          Lagers: Carlsberg, Fosters, Holsten Export.

Examples of bar/restaurant meals (lunch & evening, 7 days): *cream of broccoli soup, local smoked trout, braised pork chops with paprika & cider sauce, fresh crab cocktail, devilled kidneys, braised liver & bacon, prawns tossed in mayonnaise & rolled in smoked salmon, deep fried stilton mushrooms; half crispy duck in mango & ginger sauce, fresh salmon steak wrapped in filo pastry with dill sauce, vegetarian choices. Trad. Sun. roasts plus fish alternative. Menus revised daily.*

Well placed to benefit from nature's provenance, this fine 17th century pub draws seafood from Hastings and Rye and fresh fruits, vegetables and meats from the "Garden of England". It is then all homecooked and presented in liberal portions. One may enjoy it in the bar or two restaurants (one no-smoking), with beautiful inglenook log fires. No fruit machines, juke boxes or pool tables are to be found here; all is much as it might have been before any of them were dreamt of, right down to the flagstoned floor. Joe and Kitty Healy are relative newcomers to this establishment, taking over only in June 1991, bringing with them a wealth of experience, having spent many years in the hotel and catering trade. A hearty English breakfast awaits overnight guests. Children welcome in restaurant. Two-tier beer garden. Ample parking.

East Sussex

THE NETHERFIELD ARMS

Netherfield, nr Battle.   Tel. (042 482) 282
      Location: Village centre.
  Credit cards: Visa, Access, Mastercard.
        Bitters: Courage Best & Directors, John Smiths, Ruddles.
        Lagers: Fosters, Hofmeister, Kronenbourg.

Examples of bar meals (lunch & evening except Sun evenings in winter): *homemade soups, fried lemon sole, plaice, cod, salads, ploughman's, sandwiches, at least 8 daily specials, homemade steak & mushroom pie, steak puddings, fisherman's pie, grilled gammon steak, lasagne, curry.*
Examples of restaurant meals (as above): *fresh salmon in asparagus sauce, fresh local trout, 4 cuts of steaks, roast duckling, mixed grill, local venison, chicken Kiev, pork fillet. Vegetarian choices (8-10): healthfood salad, asparagus pancakes, mushroom stroganoff, vegetable lasagne, broccoli bake, spinach lasagne, fettucini. Homemade meringues, banana split, peach melba, luxury fruit icecreams, homemade treacle tart, bread & butter pudding, various crumbles.*

"Pub of the Year", as nominated by a local newspaper in recognition of the first rate homecooked food, and of the warm, friendly atmosphere, is a tribute to the 17 years in which Sandra and Richard Palmer have established their pretty 16th- century inn as one of the choicest in the area, well worthy of our front cover. Not far from the scene of the epic Battle of Hastings, it commands wonderful views clear to Beachy Head, almost 20 miles away. One can actually sit in the huge inglenook, in which open fires crackle in winter , and there is a full quota of oak beams. Smokers and non-smokers are segregated in two separate restaurants, and vegetarians will find possibly one of the best selections in the region. Children are welcome. Bodiam Castle, Battle Abbey and the lovely town of Rye are not far.

East Sussex

THE WHITE HART

Netherfield, nr Battle. Tel. (0424) 82382/82698
            Location: Village centre, 3 miles north of Battle.
         Credit cards: Access, Amex.
              Bitters: Harveys, Youngs Special, Whitbread Best, McKewans Best.
               Lagers: Heineken, Stella Artois.

Examples of bar/restaurant meals (lunch & evening, 7 days): *homemade steak & kidney pudding, liver & bacon, chicken & ham pie, lasagne, curry, steaks, half shoulder of lamb, grilled whole plaice, poached salmon, scampi, cheesy cauliflower & potato bake, mushroom nut & butter bean casserole, salads, ploughman's, sandwiches, daily specials. Homemade apple pie, profiteroles, cheesecake, raspberry & redcurrant pie, spotted dick. Children's menu. Traditional Sun roasts with fish alternative £7.95 (3 courses).*

"A family-run business catering for families" - that is how licensees Terry and Ange Langham, with son John, describe their friendly pub cum restaurant. Children are especially well looked after: they have their own menu, a children's room and a playground in the garden. Although fairly new to The White Hart, the Langhams have 36 years experience in the trade. Thus are they able to offer such an enormous choice which is nevertheless mostly homecooked - vegetables are also fresh whenever possible. Situated in a lovely part of Sussex, the building itself is only about 90 years old but is imbued with an 'olde worlde' atmosphere. The conservatory (a no-smoking area) is, like the other rooms, beautifully furnished, and commands fine views over the Downs. Bar billiards, shove ha'penny, darts.

THE BLACK HORSE

Telham, nr Battle.   Tel. (0424) 773109

     Location: In village.
 Credit cards: Access, Visa, Mastercard, Eurocheque.
      Bitters: Shepherd Neame Masterbrew, Spitfire, Best, Bishop's Finger.
      Lagers: Hurliman, Heineken.

Examples of bar meals (lunch & evening, except Mon. evenings): *cream of watercress soup, turkey curry, casseroles, pies, liver & bacon, daily specials. Homemade apple pie.*

Examples of restaurant meals (evenings except Mon.): *dishes as above, grills, steaks, trout, fresh fish, chicken Kiev. Trad. Sun. roasts.*

The most famous battle on English soil was fought very near here, and we all know the outcome. There's no hint now of that portentous conflict in the wonderfully peaceful countryside, and nothing more to contest than a friendly game of skittles or that other French 'invader', petanque, for which there is a league. Those are two favourite pastimes at this highly reputed 18th century pub, another being the consumption of good food hospitably served, and speedily, if required. Eddie Dunford has pulled pints here for over 27 years; he and his characterful inn together engender a notably congenial atmosphere, perhaps at its best during the annual music festival. There are fine views from the garden, which has a barbecue. Car park.

East Sussex

THE SMUGGLERS

Pett Level, nr Hastings. Tel. (0424) 813491

      Location: Near Winchelsea beach.
  Credit cards: Access, Mastercard.
       Bitters: Festive, King & Barnes, Harveys Best, Websters Yorkshire.
       Lagers: Carlsberg, Stella Artois.

Examples of bar meals (lunch & evening, 7 days): *homemade steak & mushroom pie, steak & kidney pie, chicken & ham pie, cottage pie, fresh fish, salads, daily specials eg liver & bacon, chicken casserole.*
Examples of restaurant meals (evenings except Sun. & Mon.): *egg & prawns mayonnaise, homemade soups, melon boat, whitebait; steaks, chicken Kiev, Smugglers mixed grill, roast duck, fresh fish, scampi. Sweet trolley. Trad. Sun. roasts.*

The entire sea is your playground here; as the name would suggest, the inn stands right on the seafront and was indeed once a smugglers' haunt. There's the unmistakable smack of the briny inside, too, very much in the best traditions of the seaside inn - no juke boxes or electronic games. Naturally, fresh fish is brought in daily for the kitchen, but there are plenty of alternatives - homemade pies are something of a speciality in the bar, and juicy steaks in the restaurant (accompanied by a good wine list). Graham and Barbara Cooper are licensees of nine years standing; they welcome children and have a family room, plus a garden. There's much for the youngsters as well as their parents in these parts: the Sealife Aquarium at Hastings, Smugglers' caves and the historic towns of Hastings and Rye.

THE TOP O' THE HILL

Rye Hill, Rye.   Tel. (0797) 223284

- Location: ½ mile out of Rye on A268.
- Credit cards: Access, Visa.
- Accommodation: 1 single, 5 doubles, 3 twins, 1 family. Tv's, hairdryers, tea & coffee, central heating. 6 rooms en suite.
- Bitters: King & Barnes, Youngs.
- Lagers: Carlston, Carlsberg.

Examples of bar/restaurant meals (lunch & evening, 7 days): *steak & kidney pie, pork & apple marsala, seafood lasagne, steaks, chicken breast stuffed with creamy leek & stilton sauce, Chinese duck, seafood au gratin, vegetable chilli, curry, dish of the day, kid's delight. Trad. Sun. roasts.*

Without doubt, Rye (one of the cinque ports) is amongst England's loveliest towns. Less than 10 minutes walk from its cobbled streets, standing (as the name suggests) on top of a hill, this country house style inn, pretty as a picture, blends the elegant and sophisticated with the homely and informal. The restaurant, recognised as one of the leading in the area, utilises the best local seasonal game, and seafood brought in daily by the trawlers. The well appointed bedrooms have been tastefully modernised, with a cottage style annex adding six en suite (one with facilities for the disabled), affording comfort rather superior to that endured by the 200 soldiers billeted here during the Napoleonic wars! Hazel and Peter Haydon are the proud owners, who welcome children and have a garden and car park. Well placed for superb beaches and countryside.

KENT

THE ROSE & CROWN INN

Old Romney.   Tel. (0679) 67500
        Location: Just off A259 2 miles west of New Romney.
 Accommodation: 5 twins in chalets. En suite, cntrl htng, tv's, tea & coffee.
         Bitters: Greene King IPA & Abbot, guests.
         Lagers: Kronenbourg, Castlemaine.

Examples from lunch menu (7 days): *homemade soups, chilli, shepherd's pie, chicken broccoli & potato bake, quiches, marshman's lunches, huge filled rolls. Trad. Sun. roasts.* Evening: *Spanish prawns, chicken Singapore, moussaka, salmon steak, char-grilled steaks, vegetarian dishes.*

Romney Marshes form a unique corner of Kent, strange and hauntingly beautiful. They are also famous for producing some of the best lamb in the world, quantities of which find their way to the tables of this characterful smugglers' inn, along with prime Kentish fruit and vegetables. Standing in lovely peaceful gardens, the building dates from 1689, but recently underwent a total transformation (for the better) under the auspices of Terry and Lyn Carter with partner Brian Hayes. They welcome children and the garden has play areas and barbecue. Darts, crib and shove ha'penny are indoor entertainments. For those with a taste for vast skies and the eerie silence of this landscape, the inn is ideal as a base; wonderful walks, angling and wildlife are all on your doorstep. Facilities for functions.

THE CROWN INN

Stone-in-Oxney, nr Tenterden.　　　　　　　　　　　Tel. (0233) 83789
　　　　Location: Village centre.
　　Credit cards: Not accepted.
　　　　 Bitters: Batemans, Harveys, Bass, Worthington.
　　　　 Lagers: Carling, Tennents Extra.

Examples from lunch menu (Sat & Sun): *steaks, plaice, tuna steaks, scampi, vegetarian lasagne, bean casserole, nut lasagne, omelettes.*
Evening menu (last orders 9:30pm): *homemade steak & kidney pie, steak & mushroom pie, steaks, fresh fish, many dishes as above, daily specials. Trad. Sun. roasts.*

In an exquisite setting in the heart of rural Kent, here is an authentic, unspoilt country pub of the kind we all love to chance upon whilst out for a spin through the leafy lanes. Its origins are uncertain but must be at latest 17th century, witnessed by sturdy oak beams, inglenook and, it seems, a number of spirits understandably reluctant to depart! No jukebox breaches the peace, although live jazz is planned for some evenings. Darts and cribbage are the traditional indoor pursuits, while outside there's a very pretty garden with play equipment and barbecues in season. Children are permitted inside, where there are two bars and a separate dining room. Licensees Marion and John Morris present good, wholesome food at unbeatable prices: a full four course meal on Friday and Saturday will currently set you back from just £7.50! Rye Steam Railway and many other attractions are nearby.

LA ROMANCE

57 High Street, Rolvenden.   Tel. (0580) 241992
         Location: Village centre.
      Credit cards: Access, Visa, Mastercard.

Examples from menus (lunch & evening except Mondays): *cheese fondues for 2, moules provencales, vegetable pate; poulet Romance (strips of chicken supreme sauted in olive oil, served in creamy white wine & mustard sauce), entrecote chasseur, sole meuniere/mornay, crepe gratinee (pancake filled with avocado, sultanas, cashews, onions), Scottish fillet in green peppercorn & cream sauce.*

Although not a pub, La Romance, as one of the best places to eat in the area, is worth making an exception for. And the name is fitting enough: 17th century, the cottage is quite charming, and one has the opportunity to dine al fresco in an enchantingly-lit garden terrace with flowers and music. Your hosts are Jean-Pierre and Georgina; Jean-Pierre is the chef, and he favours fresh local produce in his French cuisine. Vegetarian dishes are very much a speciality, well represented on the a la carte. The wine list, personally selected to complement the menu, is of course mostly French with one or two German and Italians, and modestly priced. So, too, is the food: expect to pay around £12 - £15 for three-course a la carte. Children welcome. No smoking area.

THE ROYAL OAK

Iden Green, nr Benenden.   Tel. (0580) 240585
     Location: In village.
 Credit cards: Access, Visa, Diners, Amex.
      Bitters: Youngs, Harveys, guest.
      Lagers: Red Stripe, Castlemaine, Carlsberg.

Examples of bar/restaurant meals (lunch & evening, 7 days): *bouillabaise, fresh grilled sardines, avocado with Waldorf salad; trad. fish & chips, skate with black butter or capers, rolls of monkfish on white wine & cream sauce, fresh salmon en croute, daily fish specialities, homemade steak & kidney pudding, maigret of duck, medallions of pork with apricot sauce, steaks, vegetarian canneloni, mushroom stroganoff. Bombe Alaska, crepes suzettes. Trad. Sun. roasts. Salad Bar. Champagne & oyster bar.*

Fish has experienced a surge in popularity in recent years, no doubt in part due to health-consciousness and also because it tastes delicious, if fresh and prepared properly. One of the county's leading exponents, The Royal Oak (ably managed by Christine Carr) features seafood very much to the fore, but at the same times offers a full complement of alternatives, including a separate vegetarian menu, all accompanied by an exceptionally good wine list. On top of this there's a salad bar displaying cold homecooked meats and, most uncommonly, a champagne and oyster bar for a special treat. If this were not enough, there are also special event evenings with themes such as French or Italian. Youngsters are welcome in the restaurant and there is a garden and children's farm.

Kent

THE GLOBE & RAINBOW INN

Kilndown, nr Goudhurst. Tel. (0892) 890283
Location: ½ mile off A21.
Credit cards: Visa, Amex.
Accommodation: 6 double/family. Some en suite, tv's, cntrl htng, fine views.
Bitters: Youngs, Flowers, Harveys, Whitbreads.
Lagers: Heineken, Stella Export.

Examples of bar meals (lunch & evening, 7 days): *homemade steak & kidney pie, other savoury pies, fresh fish, pizzas, vegetarian dishes, ploughman's, salads.*
Examples of restaurant meals (lunch & evening, Tues - Sun): *egg mornay, roast poussin stuffed with rice & sultanas, tournedos Dijon, pork cutlet in apricot & cider sauce, Dover sole with herb butter in cucumber & fennel sauce, salmon au papier, Sonny's pie of the month. Various desserts. Trad. Sun. roasts. Menus revised monthly.*

The peculiar and surely unique name is attributed to Lord Beresford-Hope, a general at the battle of Waterloo. The inn was already celebrating 100 years in business as Napolean was defeated, and the same timbers still shore it up - a truly unspoilt pub, a dwindling breed. One previous landlord liked it so much that he has apparently forsaken the afterlife to remain here! A newly converted barn houses the restaurant and the gardens (with barbecue and play area) are delightful, but it is the wide range of homecooked food which most draws custom. Proprietor John Martin supervises personally, aided by his 'team'. Combine your visit with a look over Scotney Castle or Batemans (Kipling's home). Bewl Water is also very near, as is the lovely Bedgebury Pinetum.

THE BROWN TROUT

The Down, Lamberhurst.   Tel. (0892) 890312

      Location: On B2169, almost opposite Scotney Castle.
 Credit cards: Access, Visa.
       Bitters: Flowers.
        Lagers: Heineken, Heineken Export, Stella Artois.

Examples of bar/restaurant meals (lunch & evening, 7 days): *calamari in crispy batter, deep fried mushrooms filled with cheese & garlic, lobster thermidor, wing of skate, grilled brill/halibut steak, venison in red wine sauce, chicken Kiev, steaks, ploughman's, sandwiches, daily specials. Fruit icecreams, spotted dick, treacle sponge. Trad. Sun. roasts.*

This exceptionally pretty pub is also one of the most popular in the area, so be advised to book well ahead if planning to dine on a Saturday evening. The reason is not hard to see: a varied and extensive choice of good food, served in generous portions, yet reasonably priced (the set menu from Sunday to Friday is just £9.95 for three courses and coffee). It's also a very pleasant spot to just quietly sup ale. Cottage origins are unmistakable, with a large inglenook and beams and lattices bedecked with brasses and prints (mostly depicting trout fishing). The noble fish naturally appears on the menu, and may be enjoyed in either bar or restaurant. On your way to the latter you may like to view a very fine tropical aquarium. The atmosphere is relaxed, the staff helpful, and landlord Jo Stringer permits children - the garden has swings and trampoline. Superb example of oast houses just opposite.

THE GUN & SPITROAST INN

The Heath, Horsmonden, nr Tonbridge. Tel: (0892) 722925
- Location: Village centre, opposite green
- Credit Cards: Access, Mastercard, Diners
- Bitters: Friary Meux Best, Wadworth 6X, Burton, Tetley
- Lagers: Lowenbrau, Skol

Examples of bar/restaurant meals (lunchtime 7 days, evening Tues – Sat): *homemade steak & mushroom pie, beef in red wine sauce, cold spitroasts, bacon onion & apple pie, liver & onions, chicken in port wine sauce, rump steak, chilli, lasagne, baked smokies, scampi, vegetable pasta bake, curried eggs, ploughman's, sandwiches, daily specials. Chocolate roulade, apricot sponge, sherry trifle. Trad. Sunday roasts.*

For stimulating the taste buds nothing quite compares to a spit roast turning over a crackling fire, especially in the depths of winter. Fulfilling the promise of its name, this 15th-century inn puts its inglenook to the best possible use, and the restaurant is often filled with the delicious aroma of succulent roasting pork or beef. Smokers and non-smokers are separated in two dining rooms. The main bar also has a fireplace, and both bar and restaurant are oak-beamed. Children are welcome, and the garden has a boules court. Look out for occasional special evenings. In the heart of the lovely Weald of Kent, The Gun & Spitroast epitomises so much of what is best in a traditional country inn; your first visit is unlikely to be your last. Having a function room, it is also a most suitable retreat for a business meeting or private party.

THE BULL INN

The Street, Sissinghurst.   Tel. (0580) 712821

Location:	Village centre.
Credit cards:	Visa, Mastercard.
Accommodation:	4 doubles, all en suite. £25 single, £40 double. Special breaks.
Bitters:	Flowers, Sussex, Fremlins.
Lagers:	Heineken Export, Stella Artois.

Examples of bar/restaurant meals (lunch & evening, 7 days): *Italian specialities - 20 various homemade pastas & pizzas, steak dishes (eg bistecca alla pizzaiola), 6 veal dishes, many fish dishes. Daily specials. Trad. Sun. roasts £8.95.*

One of the region's best known and most ancient villages, Sissinghurst proclaims two major attractions: Sissinghurst Castle and its lovely gardens and this handsome 14th century inn, itself with a large and beautiful garden. In this most English of settings one finds a little corner of Italy; proprietors Fedele and Theresa Russo are welll known for their first class Italian cuisine, listed on an enormous menu and accompanied by over 30 wines. Prices are astonishingly moderate: a full pasta dish costs about £5, an average three course dinner about £9 and lunch from £1.80 to £4.90. Even with 76 covers, it is no surprise that the restaurant is often quite full. For yet more diversity look out for the occasional Gourmet Evenings. Children are of course welcome. Among other places of interest in these parts is the small town of Cranbrook, with its famous windmill and delightful shops.

THE KING'S ARMS

1 High Street, Headcorn.   Tel. (0622) 890216

          Location: Village centre.
      Credit cards: Not accepted.
    Accommodation: 2 doubles, 1 twin. Cntrl htng, tea & coff. £34 per room.
            Bitters: Fremlins, Flowers IPA & Original, Harveys.
             Lagers: Stella Artois, Heineken, Heineken Export.

Examples of bar/restaurant meals (lunch & evening, 7 days): *fresh dressed crab, shell-on prawns in garlic, salmon steak, cod, grilled fresh sardines, home-baked gammon, beef stroganoff, fresh plaice with prawn & cheese sauce, steak & kidney pie. Trad. Sun. roasts (booking advised).*

Jazz lovers should keep their Friday evenings free, for that is when many of the top names in the business perform live at this super venue. Solo or duo artists play every Wednesday evening in the main bar, mostly popular music from the 50's, 60's and 70's. Once the haunt of smugglers, this attractive 16th-century inn is celebrated not only for exciting musical soirees, but also for outstanding fresh and home prepared food; so much so, in fact, that it was necessary to extend the restaurant to almost double its former size. The menu varies daily, with fresh fish always strongly featured, including sardines, a house speciality. Graham and Ann Moore have earned their success over 22 years here, which is quite exceptional in a trade becoming increasingly transient. They welcome children, and have a nice garden where barbecues are held in summer. Car park. Beautiful Leeds Castle nearby.

THE SHANT HOTEL & PRINCE OF WALES

East Sutton, nr Maidstone. Tel. (0622) 842235

- Location: 1 mile off A274.
- Credit cards: Access, Visa, Amex.
- Accommodation: 2 singles, 13 doubles, 1 twin. All en suite, col. tv's, tea coffee.
- Bitters: At least 6 real ales.
- Lagers: Hurlimanns, Stella Artois, Fosters, Heineken.

Examples of bar/restaurant meals (lunch & evening, 7 days): *filo pastry stuffed with cottage cheese & peaches on raspberry sauce, mussels in cream sauce; fillet steak stuffed with prawns & mushrooms in red wine & mushrom sauce, chicken breast with mango in cream & almond sauce, daily fresh fish, steak & kidney pudding, braised oxtails, salads, ploughman's, sandwiches. Homemade cakes & pastries. Trad. Sun. roasts.*

Situated on the edge of the Weald but with easy access to the industrial areas of north Kent, this 18th-century hotel is equally well suited to the business person as to those seeking to explore the lovely 'Garden of England'. In the eight years and more since they took over, Colin and Sue Botley have consolidated the advantages of position by striving for ever higher standards, both of the comfortable, well equipped bedrooms and in the kitchen. The choice is always extensive yet the food always fresh. Fish is bought in daily, for example, and a mouthwatering range of sweets emanates from the in-house patisserie. There's also that warm, personal service which is the hallmark of the best family-run concerns. The hotel has facilities for every kind of function, business or pleasure, and The Prince of Wales is an inn within, an alternative to eating in the restaurant. Handy for Leeds and Sissinghurst Castles.

THE PLOUGH INN

Sutton Road, Langley, nr Maidstone.　　　　　　　　Tel. (0622) 842159
　　　　Location:　A274 near Sutton Valence.
　　Credit cards:　Visa, Mastercard.
　　　　　Bitters:　Courage Directors & Best, Youngers, Theakstons XB.
　　　　　Lagers:　Kronenbourg, Hofmeister, Fosters.

Examples of bar meals (lunch & evening, 7 days): *steak & kidney pie, liver & bacon casserole, chilli, curry, Mexican chicken, fresh fish daily, evening specials eg entrecote steaks, seafood parcel. Trad. Sun. roasts (with alternatives) £8.25.*

Leeds Castle, said to be the world's most beautiful, is very near here. If England is celebrated for her stately and ancient buildings, she is even more so for traditional country pubs, of which The Plough is a fine example. We are happy to adopt traditions from other lands, so that popular dishes such as chilli or curry have become as familiar as steak and kidney pie. You will find these and much more on the menu, home cooked and very inexpensive, to be enjoyed either in the bar or dining room. The inn itself dates from the reign of Charles II (1683) and was a farm house. Modernisation has been carried out with due regard to the venerable character, and the atmosphere remains friendly and unspoilt. Jean and Ray Meredith are your hosts, and attend personally to customers. They welcome children and have a play area and barbecue in the garden. Car park.

THE RINGLESTONE INN

Ringlestone, nr Harrietsham.   Tel. (0622) 859900
      Location: Jncn 8 (Leeds Castle) off M20, B2163 toward Sittingbourne,
                     turn east at watertower north of Hollingbourne towards
                     Doddington, straight ahead at next crossroads.
  Credit cards: Access, Visa, Diners, Amex.
        Bitters: Everchanging selection of eight.
        Lagers: Everchanging selection of six.

Examples from lunchtime buffet (7 days): *lamb & stilton pie, cod & prawn fish bake, spiced chicken casserole, lamb & coconut curry, salads. Brandy bread pudding, fruit crumble, treacle nut tart, homemade cheesecake.* Examples from evening menu (7 days): *some dishes as above, rump steak in red wine sauce, grilled plaice topped with mango chutney & bananas, pork spare ribs in barbecue sauce, pizza pie, lasagne, chilli, jacket potatoes, ploughman's. Clotted cream icecreams.*

"A Ryghte Joyouse and welcome greetynge to ye all" says the inscription carved in 1632 on the oak sideboard. A previous notorious landlady took this to mean waving a shotgun at any stranger to whom she did not take a fancy, but fortunately the current landlord (for nine years) is rather friendlier. Otherwise much of the inn has changed little since it was built as a monks' hospice in 1533, and the massive dark timbers and well worn brick floors are clearly original. It is hard to credit that it stood on a busy thoroughfare, for it is now very much off the beaten track. One concession to the 20th century is the excellent lunchtime buffet, well suited to people in a hurry. Supervised children welcome, and the lovely two-acre garden has waterfalls and ample seating. Private parties arranged.

THE FLYING HORSE INN

Boughton Aluph, nr Ashford.   Tel. (0233) 620914

          Location: On village green.
    Credit cards: Access, Visa.
Accommodation: 3 doubles, 1 twin. Tv's, cntrl htng. From £30 b & b.
           Bitters: Courage Best & Directors, guest.
           Lagers: Fosters, Kronenbourg.

Examples of bar/restaurant meals (lunch & evening, 7 days): *homemade steak & kidney pie, Russian fish pie, fresh poached salmon in tarragon sauce, grilled whole local plaice, liver & bacon, lasagne. Banana & yoghurt cheesecake, death by chocolate, fruit crumble. Trad. Sun. roasts.*

The thwack of leather on willow is one of summer's most delightful sounds (except to the bowler, perhaps), and it has been heard here for over 250 years. Generations of cricketers have repaired to this much loved inn, but since the 15th century pilgrims to Canterbury have sought refreshment, for it stands on the Pilgrims' Way. Over the past five years Howard and Christine Smith have maintained this long record of hospitality, having 12 previous successful years of innkeeping. Food is better than ever, always fresh and home cooked, and the menu revised daily. Brasses catch the glow of open fires in winter, and fresh flowers grace the single pleasant bar all year. Bat and Trap (a Kentish game) is played in the garden, as is jazz in kind weather - barbecues, too. Children permitted in certain areas. Booking advised for rooms. Dining room let for functions.

Kent

THE TIGER INN

Stowting, nr Ashford. Tel. (0303) 862130/862278
Location: Off B2068 Hythe to Canterbury road.
Credit cards: Access, Visa.
Bitters: Everards Tiger, Greene King Abbot, Wadworth, Burtons, Tetley.
Lagers: Lowenbrau, Stella Artois, Castlemaine.

Examples of bar meals (lunch & evening, 7 days): *homemade steak kidney & mushroom pie, cheesy smoked haddock & prawn pie (both noted), local trout, plaice, vegetarian choices, daily specials. Banana & Malibu nests, apple pie.*
Examples of restaurant meals (as above): *rack of lamb baked in breadcrumbs & herbs, poached wild salmon with dill & cream, mallard with bitter orange & brandy sauce, pheasant with green apples in cointreau & cream sauce. Brandy snaps with vanilla icecream covered in brandy & ginger sauce. Trad. Sun. roasts in winter.*

At the foot of the North Downs, this homely 17th-century inn is well placed for walkers and anyone who loves the lush, rolling countryside. In summer one can bask on the sunny terrace, in winter snuggle up to the fire, but do try the food - well above the norm, and a good range of beers, too. Menus are revised continually to reflect what is fresh and seasonal. The bar is redolent of a farmhouse kitchen, with posies of flowers, plates on the dresser and a scattering of cushions. The candlelit restaurant seats up to 30 and is bookable for private parties. Monday is jazz night, attended by other landlords on their night off, and red letter days like Halloween or New Year are marked by fancy dress do's. Alan and Linda Harris welcome well behaved children and organise weekend barbecues, weather permitting.

Kent

THE DOLLS HOUSE

Elham Valley Road, Barham, nr Canterbury.　　　　Tel. (0227) 831241
      Location: On B2065, middle of Elham Valley.
   Credit cards: Access, Visa.
       Bitters: Shepherd Neame Master Brew, Wadworth 6X, John Smiths, guests.
       Lagers: Stella Artois, Carling, Fosters, Heineken, Heineken Export, Tennents LA.

Examples of bar/restaurant meals (lunch & evening, 7 days): *homemade soups & pates, homemade pies (eg rabbit & cider, chicken & oyster), breast of duck with marmalade sauce, mushroom & onion stroganoff, daily specials. Trad. Sun. roasts.*

Recommended by Egon Ronay, here is a prime example of how pub food has improved over recent years. The enormously varied menus are changed regularly, and served with friendly informality in spotlessly clean surrounds. The exposed beams and inglenooks in lounge bar and two cottagey dining rooms indicate 17th century origins, but the name derives from the many dolls made by the mother of a previous landlord. Unfortunately they were destroyed (only pictures remain), and there are stories of unexplained 'bangs' in the night and objects moved. Children are welcome, and there's a large landscaped garden. Small parties and meetings catered for. Vineyard adjoins pub. Dover, Canterbury and Howletts Zoo all within easy reach.

Kent

THE BLAZING DONKEY

Hay Hill, Ham, nr Sandwich.   Tel. (0304) 617362
        Location: Off A256 from Eastry.
    Credit cards: Access, Visa, Diners.
         Bitters: Tetleys, Burtons, Master Brew, John Bull, King & Barnes.
         Lagers: Various, Kaliber LA. Plus Addlestones & Old English ciders

Examples of bar meals (lunch & evening, except Sun evening): *chicken tikka, lasagne, curries, cottage pie, ploughman's, salads.*
Examples of restaurant meals (lunch & evening, trad. Sun. lunch): *steaks with pepper or Madeira sauce, chicken supreme with garlic butter coated in fresh breadcrumbs (or with cream, wine & mushroom sauce), trout, salmon steak in red wine, vegetarian dishes, all served with chef's choice of potato & fresh vegetables.*

Fresh produce for the kitchen is grown in the pub's own greenhouse, and the landscaped garden/patio is exceptionally large and well maintained. One side of the 300-year-old building is covered in a colourful mural, and extensions and modernisations have been taste fully executed. The single bar has been furnished in cottage style, and the 90 seater dining room can serve equally as a function room for weddings and private parties. Country and Western, folk and jazz are performed live on a regular basis. Barbecues are served Sunday lunchtimes and Saturday, weather permitting. The management welcomes children (and dogs) if well behaved, and the play area has swings, slide and bouncy castle.

THE ANCHOR INN

2 Beakesbourne Lane, Littlebourne, nr Canterbury.   Tel. (0227) 721207
- Location: Centre of village.
- Credit cards: Not accepted.
- Accommodation: Planned.
- Bitters: Flowers, Fremlins, Whitbread.
- Lagers: Heineken Export, Stella Artois.

Examples of bar meals (lunch & evening, 7 days): *homemade pies (eg ham & leek, steak & Guinness, chicken & mushroom), steak & kidney pudding, jacket potatoes, baguettes, ploughman's, sandwiches.*

Examples of restaurant meals (as above): *homemade soup, deep fried brie, seafood platter, whitebait; lamb cutlets, scampi, gammon steaks, salmon steak, steaks, daily specials.*

The name does not, as you might think, have nautical connections, but in fact derives from 'Anker', an old continental measure of beer equivalent to eight and one third imperial gallons. The Anker House, as it was once known, began in 1623, in the reign of Charles I, has been a courthouse in its time, but it is now put to much better use as a fine country pub with separate a la carte restaurant on two storeys. Upstairs is a lovely pine dining room, downstairs was converted from a stable and is full of atmosphere. This is licensees Jackie and Tony Bessant's first venture of this kind, and they have not long been here, but already they have plans to add accommodation - a real asset so close to Canterbury. Children welcome. Garden and large car park.

THE OLDE GATE INN & RESTAURANT

162 New Dover Road, Canterbury.   Tel. (0227) 452154

Location:	Off old A2 - main access road from Dover.
Credit cards:	Access, Visa, Amex.
Accommodation:	8 doubles, 1 family (en suite), 1 single. TV, hair dryer, trouser press, tea-making, dbl-glazing. From £40 per room.
Bitters:	Ruddles, John Smith, Websters.
Lagers:	Carlsberg, Kronenbourg.

Examples of bar meals (lunch & evening, except Sun evening): *wide selection includes shepherd's pie, steak & kidney pie, fresh fish speciality dishes.*
Examples of restaurant meals: *carvery every day except Mon, wide choice of roast joints, plus other dishes.*

On 1½ prime acres, site of the original tollgate straddling Watling Street (one of the great Roman roads in Britain), The Olde Gate is a stylish blend of small hotel, Kentish pub and light, airy carvery restaurant (with agreeable sun terrace). Complete refurbishment has successfully recreated a Victorian 'country style' ambience, but with a distinctive cosmopolitan flavour, for Canterbury of course attracts many foreign visitors. Chris and Sandy Gear are friendly hosts; they welcome children if eating and have a garden. Parking for 60 is a major asset, and the county cricket ground is nearby. The new bedrooms are furnished to a very high standard, harmonising soft pine furniture with pastel colours and fabrics, and affording a panorama over the orchards of Kent - well suited for business or pleasure.

The Ship Inn and Smugglers Restaurant

THE SHIP INN & SMUGGLERS RESTAURANT

Conyer, Teynham, nr Sittingbourne. Tel. (0795) 521404

      Location: Waterside, 2 miles from A2, signposted from Teynham.
   Credit cards: Access, Visa.
       Bitters: 5 handpumps changed continually: Adnams, Batemans, Boddingtons, Brakspears, Camerons, Chas Wells, Courage Directors, Eldridge Pope, Everards, Fremlins, Flowers, Fullers, Gales, Goachers, Greene King, Harveys, King & Barnes Marstons, Ruddles, Shepherd Neame, Theakstons, Wadworth, Whitbread, Youngers, Youngs.
       Lagers: 9 taps rotating: Becks, Budweiser, Carlsberg, Grolsch, Heineken, Heineken Export, Holsten, Hurlimann, Kronenbourg, Lowenbrau, Moosehead, Stella Artois. Plus Biddenden cider.

Examples of bar meals (lunch & evening, 7 days): *local oysters, dressed crab, rainbow trout, homemade pies, curry, chilli, vegetarian dishes, wide range of ploughman's, toasted sandwiches, deep fried basket meals.*
Examples of restaurant meals (as above): *lobster thermidor, Dover sole, many steak dishes, wide range of seafood platters, moules mariniere, swordfish, game, daily specials.*

Built in the reign of Charles I, the inn was the centre of local smuggling activities over two centuries, in this little backwater off the Swale as in a hundred other quiet creeks along the Kent coast. The Smugglers Restaurant captures something of the spirit of those times, and 'The Dungeon' and 'Smugglers Store' dining areas are invested with a unique atmosphere. Of the extensive menu, it was the editor of 'Food & Drink' magazine who wrote, "In truth, I have had but a handful of memorable visits to table in 20 years of following the dubious profession of eating for a living. On the day of my visit to The Ship Inn & Smugglers Restaurant, I had one of the most memorable meals of my life."

The good food and wide range of dishes available both as bar snacks and in the restaurant is supported by a truly magnificent wine list, for which Alec and Lindsay Heard have received three major awards. The most recent of these was Les Routiers' 'Mercier Champagne Corps d'Elite 1991' award for outstanding wine list. Customers preferring beer as their beverage will have chosen well in seeking out this little creekside watering hole. Beside the range of draught beers and lagers there is a collection of more than 50 bottled beers from around the world to try. With 250 whiskies, 150 liqueurs, 50 brandies, 50 rums and a wide range of ports, for the connoisseur and novice alike, this is a most remarkable hostelry. In a word, it is unsurpassed for choice in the county.

Kent

THE RED LION

Hernhill, nr Faversham.   Tel. (0227) 751207
        Location: On village green, not far off M2.
    Credit cards: Access, Visa.
          Bitters: Shepherd Neame Master Brew, Fullers London Pride, Marston's Pedigree.
           Lagers: Hurlimanns, Heineken. Plus Theobalds cider.

Examples of bar meals (lunch & evening, 7 days): *curry, scampi, spaghetti bolognese, Yorkshire pudding with steak & kidney filling, lion burger, chilli, omelettes, salads, ploughman's, sandwiches, daily specials eg chicken in white wine sauce.*
Examples of restaurant meals (lunch & evening except Mons): *trout filled with prawns, butterfly chicken, pork chops in apple & calvados sauce, sirloin steak, Dover sole, vegetarian dish. Trad. Sun. roasts.*

Here is a dream of an English village: the church on one side of the green, a lovely old timbered pub on the other. Landlord Michael White revitalised the latter, opening for business in December 1990. Holding up the entire edifice is a king post, quite rare, and visible in the upstairs restaurant - a splendid room, thickly carpeted, with vaulted ceiling and giant potted plants, suitable for a wedding reception etc. The bar has both woodblock and flagstoned floors, fine exposed brickwork and timbers, and log fires. 'Obadiah', a deceased ex-landlord is said to walk, but seems to trouble nobody. A pianist tickles the ivories on Fridays, and there's usually other entertainment on Tuesdays. The large garden has a play area (children also welcome inside), bat-and-trap and petanque under the walnut tree. Barbecues held Sundays and bank holidays.

THE LEATHER BOTTLE

The Street, Cobham, nr Gravesend. Tel. (0474) 814327

    Location: Village centre, on main road.
  Credit cards: Access, Visa, Diners, Amex.
 Accommodation: 2 singles, 2 doubles, 1 twin, 2 4-posters. Some en suite, all with good facilities. From £37 sngl, £54 dbl. Special weekend breaks.
     Bitters: Ruddles County, Websters.
     Lagers: Carlsberg, Holsten Export, Kaliber.

Examples of bar meals (lunch & evening, 7 days): *beef & Guinness, roast topside, homemade shepherds pie, ham & mushroom pie, vegetable bake, salad bar.*
Examples of restaurant meals (as above): *steaks, chicken & stilton roulade, lemon sole with prawn sauce, medallions of pork finished in light cream & white wine sauce, rainbow trout in almonds. Trad. Sun. roasts.*

Dickens made mention of this lovely old inn in 'Pickwick Papers', and drank here himself - Dickens memorabilia is everywhere, generating the atmosphere of those times. It precedes him by several centuries (built 1629), and was a royalist meeting place during the Civil War. It acquired its name when a leather bottle containing gold sovereigns was found around 1720. Landlord Michael Eakins and staff welcome children, and in the large garden is 'Bumbles Teashop', open Sundays and Bank Hols. This is a marvellous spot for a stay, being quietly situated just minutes from the M2. Just opposite is Cobham Church, considered to be the best in the country for brass rubbings, and Cobham Hall is an easy walk.

THE ROSE & CROWN

Stone Street, nr Seal, Sevenoaks. Tel. (0732) 810233
    Location: Centre of hamlet of Stone Street, between Seal and Ivy Hatch.
    Credit cards: Not accepted.
    Bitters: Fremlins, Flowers, Harveys.
    Lagers: Stella Artois, Heineken.

Examples of bar/restaurant meals (lunch & evening, 7 days. Limited menu Mondays): *parma ham with melon, seasonal specialities (incl.game), smoked fish platter (noted), crab soup, skate, plaice, chicken chasseur, rack of lamb, guinea fowl, tender farm duck (prepared by delicious secret method), veal kidneys giannini, mussels, entrecote pizzaiola, steaks, ratatouille, daily specials. Zabaglione & other homemade desserts.*

For quality homecooked food, seek out this little gem, lost in the depths of the countryside, just off the A225. Naturally, all is fresh and varies according to season; expect to find hare, venison etc in winter, and fresh shellfish in summer. The menu blends English and continental cuisine, with perhaps an Italian accent - Luigi and Debbie Carugati are the proprietors. Essentially this is a quiet, unspoilt country pub, undisturbed by juke boxes or indoor games. Children are welcome, of course, and there's a large sunny garden. Apple orchards present a pleasant aspect to the front, and Ightham Mote is a nearby attraction. Large car park.

Others in this series.

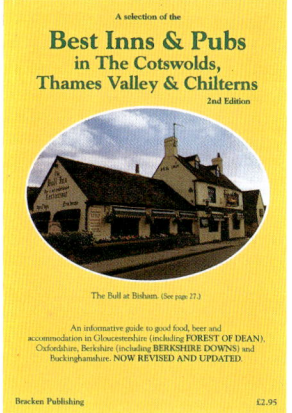

£3.50

£3.50

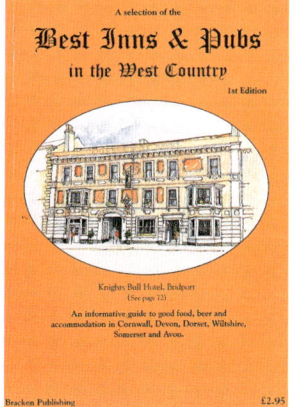

£3.50

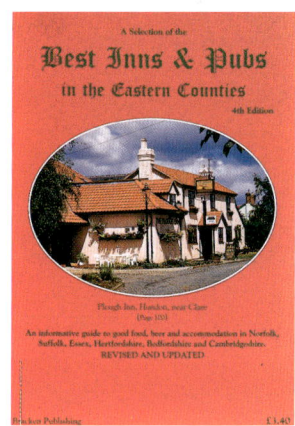

£4.00

Also published: Best Hotels & Restaurants in the Eastern Counties (£3.50)
Your Garden in East Anglia (£4.00)

Available in most bookshops and some pubs within the area, or by writing to Bracken Publishing. No orders will be accepted without prior payment, other than from recognised retailers.

Above prices include postage etc

LOCATOR MAP
Hampshire, Surrey and West Sussex

Towns bracketed are not featured in guide.
⊙ accommodation

LOCATOR MAP
Surrey, West Sussex, East Sussex and Kent

Towns bracketed are not featured in guide.
⊙ accommodation

INDEX

Hampshire

- * Alresford, Swan Hotel 26
- Bentley, Star Inn..24
- Boldre, Red Lion..37
- Chawton, Greyfriar...25
- * Cheriton, Flower Pots Inn 43
- Dummer, Queen Inn 29
- Dundridge, Hampshire Bowman 42
- * East Stratton, Plough Inn 28
- Ellisfield, Fox 23
- * Emery Down, New Forest Inn 38
- Freefolk Priors, Watership Down Inn.........................30
- Hambledon (Broadhalfpenny Down), Bat & Ball 41
- Hartley Wintney, Phoenix 19
- Hawkley, Hawkley Inn 44
- Hook, Crooked Billet 21
- Lymington, Champagne Charlies 36
- Newnham, Old house at Home 20
- North Warnborough, Swan 22
- Ovington, Bush Inn 27
- Portsmouth, George Inn..40
- Romsey, Old House at Home 39
- Sopley, Woolpack Inn..35
- * Stockbridge, White Hart Inn 33
- Vernham Dean, George Inn 32
- Whitsbury, Cartwheel Inn 34
- Wolverton (Townsend), George & Dragon 31

Kent

- Barham, Dolls House 90
- * Boughton Aluph, Flying Horse Inn 88
- * Canterbury, Olde Gate Inn & Restaurant 93
- * Cobham, Leather Bottle...97
- Conyer, Ship Inn 95
- * East Sutton, Shant Hotel & Prince of Wales.............85

* accommodation

INDEX

Kent *(continured)*

   Ham, Blazing Donkey 91
* Headcorn, King's Arms 84
   Hernhill, Red Lion 96
   Horsmonden, Gun & Spitroast 82
   Iden Green, Royal Oak 79
   Kilndown, Globe & Rainbow Inn 80
   Lamberhurst, Brown Trout 81
   Langley, Plough Inn 86
* Littlebourne, Anchor Inn 92
* Old Romney, Rose & Crown 76
   Ringlestone, Ringlestone Inn 87
   Rolvenden, La Romance 78
   Seal (Stone Street), Rose & Crown 98
* Sissinghurst, Bull Inn 83
   Stone-in-Oxney, Crown Inn 77
   Stowting, Tiger Inn 89

Surrey

   Bagshot, White Hart 13
   Blackwater, Lamb 14
* Chiddingfold, Crown Inn 7
   Chobham, Cricketers 12
   Downside, Cricketers 9
   Farnham (Boundstone), Bat & Ball 15
* Felbridge, Woodcock Inn 4
* Frensham (Millbridge), Mariners Hotel 17
   Frensham (Shortfield Common), Hollybush 18
   Ockley, Cricketers Arms 6
   Ottershaw, Castle Inn 11
   Outwood, Bell Inn 5
   Oxted (Broadham Green), Haycutter 3
   Shepperton, Thames Court 10
   Shere, Prince of Wales 8
   Tilford, Barley Mow 16

* accommodation

INDEX

Sussex

	Ansty, Ansty Cross Inn	59
	Apuldram, Black Horse	49
	Ashurst, Fountain Inn	58
	Billingshurst, Blue Ship	57
	Bucks Green, Fox Inn	55
	Burpham, George & Dragon	50
*	Chilgrove, Royal Oak	46
	Coolham, Selsey Arms	56
	Cootham, Crown Inn	51
	Crowborough, Plough & Horses	65
	Elsted, Three Horseshoes	45
	Haywards Heath, Fox & Hounds	61
	Horsted Keynes, Crown	60
	Isfield, Halfway House	63
*	Kirdford, Half Moon Inn	54
	Lewes, Pelham Arms	62
	Netherfield, Netherfield Arms	71
	Netherfield, White Hart	72
	Pett Level, Smugglers	74
*	Petworth, Angel Hotel	53
	Pevensey Bay, Star Inn	68
*	Rye, Top 'o the Hill	75
	Seaford, Golden Galleon	67
	Sheffield Green, Sheffield Coach House	64
	Stopham Bridge, White Hart	52
	Telham, Black Horse	73
*	Ticehurst, Cherry Tree	70
	Warbleton, War-Bill-In-Tun Inn	69
	West Ashling, Richmond Arms	47
	West Wittering, Lamb Inn	48
	Withyham, Dorset Arms	66

* accommodation